AF375201

Dedication

Dedication

Dedicated to my guiding angels, grandfather, (Late) Pandit Roshan Lal and brother, (Late) Ashish Bhardwaj. And also to my supportive and loving father, Jugal Kishor Sharma. Their contribution to my life is beyond words.

Dedication
Index
Acknowledgement
Getting the most out of this book
How to use this book
Introduction
23 Main chapters
Revision

Acknowledgement

First and foremost, all thanks and praises to God, who blessed me with everything I need in my life. He is the reason behind all my achievements and successes. He lifted me whenever I fell, made me stronger and better with every passing moment. He loved and cared for me unconditionally. My words will fall short of describing His role in my life.

My heartfelt gratitude to Nirmal Ma'am for having faith in me. She has constantly motivated, guided, and supported me from the time I was a college student. She saw something in me that I could not see. She ignited the spark in me and helped me to become Memory King and Vedic Maths Expert.

I would like to express my special thanks and gratitude to Sagar Dodeja Sir. He is the person who has helped me in all my ups and downs and supported me at every step of my life. He has always given me things that I required without asking for any return. My journey till here was better because of him.

I want to acknowledge and give my warmest thanks to my brother, Gajanand Sharma. His presence and words always fill me with confidence and inspire me to work harder. He has always been there when I needed him. I owe him a lot.

I am highly thankful to my uncle, Shubhas Singla, who made me stand on my feet. He treated me like his own son, even without having any blood relation. He taught me the art of sacrifice, giving without expecting, and working smartly.

I owe an enormous debt of gratitude to my beautiful, caring, and understanding wife, Khushboo Bhardwaj. My heart is filled with love and gratitude for her. She is the best example of how an ideal wife and friend should be. I am extremely thankful to her for coming into my life and filling it with colours.

I am deeply thankful to Palmeichung, who helped me in finalising this book. I truly appreciate the time and energy spent by him to provide valuable suggestions and comments. My warmest regards to him for his sincere effort.

I am immensely grateful to the editor of this book, Bhavana Vashisht, without whom my dream of finishing this book would be incomplete. She organised, edited, and wonderfully finalised this book. She is a brilliant writer and kind-hearted human. I am glad to have her on my team.

I am eternally grateful to the designer of this book, Sanjeev Saini. His hard work, creativity, and innovations completely transformed this book. He has always surprised me with his great designs. He is a gifted designer with magnificent designing skills.

Last but not least, I want to thank every reader from the bottom of my heart. Your constant showers of love and support on my online courses, YouTube videos, websites, webinars, seminars, and various other initiatives, encouraged me to write this book. I do all this for you as I want to contribute something to your life and help you achieve extraordinary success.

How to Get the Most out of this Memory Book

This is not an ordinary traditional textbook. It is a specially curated book to help you master your memory. All the chapters are arranged in a proper sequence. So, avoid skipping any chapter or studying random chapters. Whenever you start reading a new chapter, you can first read this portion. This will remind you of what you should and should not do to get the most out of this book. As it is a special book, the procedure to read and use it is also very special. To get the maximum results from this book, follow the steps mentioned here.

Identify your Why and What

Before starting to read this book, you should know why you are reading this and what you want to achieve from this book. This will motivate you throughout your journey of reading this book. In this way, you will be able to extract the most out of this book and will get the solutions easily to whatever you are seeking.

Highlight and Take Notes

Make a separate notebook to write the important ideas, examples, and concepts. Keep a pen and paper next to you while reading this book. Don't just skim through the book; take out time to note down things that will be useful for you later. You can also write short summaries of each chapter after completing it. Once you have read the entire book, you can write a short summary and review of the book. These small tasks will be highly useful to you and will stay with you for a lifetime.

Pause and Reflect

This is not the kind of book that can be completed in one go. This book has the potential to change your life. Don't keep a target to finish the book at the earliest possible time. Rather, keep a target to extract the most out of this book whatever time it may take. Take your time while reading this. Keep your purpose of reading in mind. Don't rush through the book; proceed slowly and steadily. So, don't read for the sake of reading or competing with others. Reread the text until you are clear with it. Give justice to each chapter so that the chapter can do justice to you.

Practise and Implement

This book is filled with practice sets. This is not a theoretical book rather a very practical book to achieve a super memory. I can guarantee you, if you do the practice sets given in the book and implement the techniques in real life, this book will do miracles and prove to be a game-changer. Practising the concepts is the most important thing that you need to do. Without it, your efforts and time will be a waste. Convert ideas and theories into action. The real power lies in the execution and implementation of knowledge.

Revisit and Revise

Revisiting the already read text gives you a new perspective to look at that and always teaches something new to you which you must have missed in the first reading. Revision plays a vital role in deciding your success rate. There is a scientific revision plan, by following it, you won't ever forget any information. You should ideally do at least three revisions of everything you study. The first within twenty-four hours, the second within a week, and the third within a month of studying the text. This way, you can achieve extraordinary success. Fix time to revise what you have read. The first revision can be done every night. The second revision can be done on Sundays. And, the third revision can be done on the last Sunday of the month. From my personal experience, I can say that victory can only be achieved through practice and revision.

Share and Discuss

Sharing what you have learnt is a great way to store information permanently in the brain. It not only helps the person with whom the information is being shared but also immensely helps the person who is sharing. It makes the learning process interesting and enjoyable. You can create a group of people you feel comfortable with. There, you can share and discuss what you have studied. Discussions make your concepts stronger and clearer. They boost your confidence and self-esteem. You can hold discussion sessions once in a while.

About the Book

Do you forget what you studied? Do you often forget the names of the people, important events, and schedules? Are you not able to focus on your studies and avoid distractions? Do you find it difficult to memorise complex words and long texts? Do you forget the birthdays and anniversaries dates of your loved ones? Do you want to utilise your brainpower fully? Do you want to leave a mark on this world? If your answer to any of these questions is yes, then you are at the right place.

Extraordinary Memory—Your Secret Guide To A Super Memory is made after proper analysis of common problems faced by people, especially in terms of memorisation. All the solutions related to memory can be found in this book, which is prepared after thirteen years of research. This book can be used by not only students but also professionals, home-makers, entrepreneurs, and anyone who wishes to improve their memory and performance.

This book has the potential to change your life drastically. This will not only make you a memory champion but also improve your everyday life, relations, career, and studies. Furthermore, this will motivate you to take over the world by creating world records and impressing anyone you meet.

This is a one-of-a-kind memory enhancement book, which includes:
- Colourful and brain-friendly content
- Reliable and authentic techniques
- Scientifically proven methods
- Worksheets and practice sets
- Separate study skills chapters
- Practical tips and tricks
- Motivational quotes
- Interesting images
- Revision lessons
- Short cut tricks, and much more

After completing this book, you will be able to memorise easily:
- Names of people, their phone numbers, addresses, and other details
- All elements of the periodic table, along with their specifications
- Names of countries and their capitals, parliaments, currencies, etc.
- Names of prime ministers, presidents, etc.
- Names of books and their authors
- Lengthy chapters and answers
- Important schedules and dates
- Difficult words and spellings
- Facts and figures
- And anything you want to remember

My Story

From Ordinary to Extraordinary

I would like to share my story with you, not to showcase my achievements or struggles but to inspire you and assure you that if I, being an ordinary boy from a remote area, can achieve extraordinary success then, you can as well. Along with 29 world records and 6 national records, I am an international memory and Vedic maths trainer, inventor, life coach, entrepreneur, and philanthropist. However, behind all my success, there is a lesser-known story full of struggles.

My journey till here has been full of ups and downs. In school, my teachers used to scold me for not concentrating on my studies. I used to get mocked by classmates. I was among those students who had exam phobia. I had no ambitions and considered studies very boring. Being a maths and memory expert now does not mean that I was good at them from childhood. Rather, earlier, they were like my enemies. I had a bad memory and hated maths. I had to struggle hard to remember details and pass my exams.

My family is from a village called Sallhawas in Jhajjar, Haryana. My father has now retired from the Indian Army, and my mother is a homemaker. From the beginning, conditions at home were not favourable, and we struggled hard to survive on less money and resources. In the board exams of the 10th class, I scored fewer marks and performed below average in maths. That generated a fear of maths inside me. Somehow, I completed my 12th class. But I was extremely frustrated. So, I quitted my studies and started selling newspapers for my livelihood. After seeing all this, my father became very sad and left everything, including his job, house, farm, etc., and shifted to Gurugram.

That acted as a turning point in my life. At that moment, I realised that I should do something for my father. I thought that my father had sacrificed everything for me, now it is my duty to make him proud. I had two options, first was to go on living a tearful, poor, and non-purposeful life, and the second was to overcome my fears and achieve something extraordinary. That was the time when I started believing in myself. I challenged the world and left behind all my fears. After that, I never looked back.

'Extraordinary accomplishments are only achieved when we are able to overcome extraordinary challenges.'

This is my life story in brief. What you can take away from this story is that the journey to achieve glamorous things is filled with hardships. But there is no need to fear hardships as they come to polish you. Also, no one is born a genius. But with practice and determination, you can achieve great success. You have the power to change your destiny, and everything lies in your hands.

'Success does not happen overnight.'

It takes the right amount of time, effort, sweat, smart work, and sacrifice to achieve exceptional things. Because I faced a lot of troubles, so I can very well empathise with other people. And that is the reason why I want to help everyone overcome their fears and progress in life and career.

I have included all the secrets that I used to make world records in this book. This will train you to face difficult situations and improve your overall quality of life. For you all, I will keep writing such books and keep assisting you in whatever way I can.

'Sharing is caring!
The more we give to others,
the more we receive.'

CHAPTER 1

THREE SECRET STEPS TO A SUPER MEMORY

Build a Strong Foundation for an Extraordinary Memory

'A man's real possession is his memory. In nothing else is he rich, in nothing else is he poor.'

—*Alexander Smith*

Memory is a crucial factor on which your results depend—not only in professional life but also in personal life. Cicero, a famous Roman scholar, used to define memory as 'the treasury and guardian of all things.' It is a fact that the better memory you have, the more impressed people will be with you and the better grades you will get in your exams. To have a super command over your memory, I will share three secrets with you. These secret principles are the foundation of a strong memory. To know them, remember AIR. AIR stands for Association, Imagination, and Ridiculous thinking. AIR is so powerful and effective that it can triple your memory powers. To understand it, you need to learn like a kid. Do you remember how you were when you were a kid? Yes, you were curious and always eager to learn. This quality is what you require to learn the secrets. Become a kid once again. When you hold this book, forget your titles and designations and become curious like a kid.

ASSOCIATE TO SUCCEED

ASSOCIATION

The first principle you should know to have a fantastic memory is association. Imagine association as a chain. Just like a chain is formed by joining several links. Similarly, an association is formed by joining various words, pictures, or events.

Let us understand this with an example of an elephant. You might have seen a huge elephant tied to a short and thin rope—which the elephant can easily break, but still, it doesn't. Why? To know the reason, let us go back to the time when it was a baby. At that time, it was tied to a short rope which was tied to a small pole. The youthful and energetic baby elephant wanted to explore the world and tried every day to break this rope without losing hope. He put all his energy into breaking it, but in vain. In the end, it accepted its defeat and lost hope. So, what happened in this process was that the baby elephant associated or connected that rope with itself. Unknowingly, it made a strong association in mind with that rope, and as it grew older—the association grew stronger. And when it was old enough to have the power of uprooting several trees, the elephant could not break that short, thin rope tied to a small pole. The rope was not binding the elephant. Instead, the association developed during childhood was binding it to one place.

Similarly, many people are afraid of cockroaches even after knowing that they can't do anything to a several thousand times heavier and stronger human. But do you know from where the fear originated? It started when those people were kids and used to run after cockroaches to catch them. But every time they did this, their parents stopped them by instilling fear in them and associating the cockroaches with ghosts or danger. When these people grew up, their association with cockroaches as the danger increased, which led them to believe that it will cause harm to them even at an older age. This is the power of association. It can cause a profound impact on people emotionally, mentally, and physically.

Even I used to be one of the victims of such associations. In my childhood, my grandmother used to tell me stories. One of her familiar stories was that ghosts come to scare us after 11 p.m. when we are alone in the dark. Listening to such things, I associated darkness and loneliness with ghosts and danger, and even after growing up, I could not stay late at night, fearing that ghosts will come. But due to my understanding of the memory world and association, I decided to break free of such associations.

You will be glad to know that it takes more time to build an association than to break it. The elephant can break the rope in a second if it realises this principle, and people can get free from the fear of anything if they understand the root cause of fear-association. Our happiness, sadness, success, failure, etc., all depend on association. It is so powerful that we can do miracles if we correctly apply this principle in studies or work.

Everything in this world is associated with some other thing. Suppose I say, Sachin Tendulkar, you will associate him with cricket. If I talk about Narendra Modi, you will associate him with PM or BJP. And, you will associate me, Dr. Himmat, with this book. Right? You see, all words are connected to some other words through association. Likewise, all information in the brain is connected to some other information. A fan is associated with a roof, and without a roof, a fan can't be defined. Similarly, without association, our information in the brain can't be defined. We will learn more exciting things about this in upcoming chapters.

Imagination Can Do Wonders

Our next step towards memory mastery is imagination. Albert Einstein used to say, 'Imagination is more important than knowledge.' He believed so because he knew that all inventions and great discoveries require imagination. If you understand the power of imagination, it will cause a massive positive change in your studies and work.

Imagine you have just watched a movie. Now, I ask you about the hero, heroine, dialogues, and plot. Will you be able to tell? Of course, yes! Did you notice that you can retain most of the details of the movie without notes, revision, or repetition? We did not try to memorise that; still, we remembered. But when we try to memorise some notes, we cannot remember them without putting in a lot of effort. How did this happen? It was because of imagination or visualisation that we could remember pictures and scenes easily. Also, as watching a movie involves more senses than reading notes; therefore, we can comfortably retain it.

Our brain is better at remembering pictures than words. So, it might have happened to you that you can recognise the face when you see a person but not the name. But why is it that you remember the face but not the name? It is because you saw the face and you heard the name. When we see something, the chances to remember it is twenty times higher—as it gets stored in long-term memory. Biologically, our eyes-to-brain nerve connection is stronger than ears to brain connection. That is why our visual sense is more potent than the auditory sense. Just like the olfactory (smell) sense is the strongest in dogs, the auditory sense is strongest in deer. Similarly, the visual sense is strongest in most humans.

It won't be wrong if we compare the brain with a picture dictionary. The brain stores the information received from the senses in a pictorial form. To understand it further, let us do an activity. There are some call words given in the worksheet; you have to write what comes to your mind after reading them in the response section. Before starting, remember that you don't have to picturise the image in any case. Just try to write your response without thinking of the colour, shape, place of the object mentioned. For example, when you read the first call word—monkey, your response should not be what you visualise or imagine. Similarly, try to attempt the rest of the call words.

You must have realised that you could not answer them without stopping their pictures from coming to your mind. This happens because your brain has stored all those information in a pictorial format, and by using this quality of brain, you can excel in all fields.

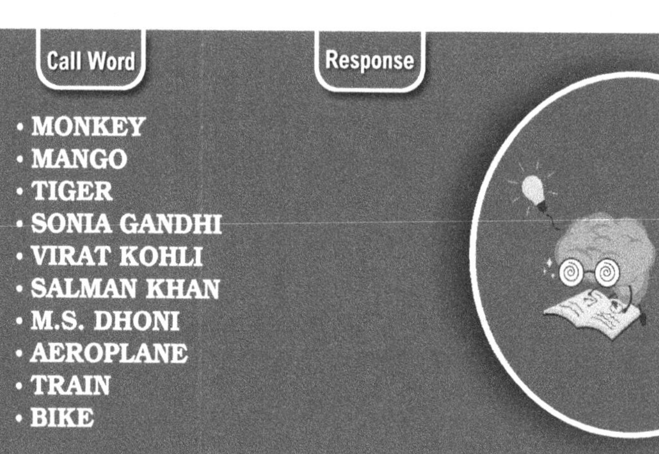

Ridiculous
Thinking is Not Ridiculous

The last secret principle to boost your memory is ridiculous thinking. For example, when a person said he is going to the moon, people around him, including his friends and family members, ridiculed him and made fun of him. But when he did go to the moon, they praised him. Also, in my case—coming from a village background, when I told people around me that I would make world records, they laughed at me and called me an illogical person with ridiculous thinking. But with my hard work, when I made 29 world records, they congratulated me. This is the power of ridiculous thinking. It may seem ridiculous at first, but it is very powerful and effective. We will learn how to use it in-depth in upcoming chapters.

Notes:

Use the AIR formula to get remarkable memory:
- Associate the new information with the old information there in your mind.
- Imagine the association that you made.
- Ridiculously visualise the association.

CHAPTER 2

MAKE UNFORGETTABLE STORIES WITH THE STORY METHOD

'Our stories have the power to break down barriers.'

—*Anonymous*

We have covered the theoretical part of AIR (Association, Imagination, and Ridiculous thinking). Now, it is time to move onto the practical part of it. The method shared with you in this chapter is highly beneficial and effective—it is called the story or chain method.

It is a powerful yet easy-to-use method to improve your memory many folds. If you master this story method, you will be able to remember a list of words or events in forward, reverse, and random sequence. Along with this, you will be able to quickly learn the names of all states, countries, currency, elements in the periodic table, or any other kind of list, without putting in a lot of effort or time. You are aware that such lists of things can't be remembered like conceptual concepts—which can be understood and learned. Instead, they have to be read again and again to memorise. From the methods taught to you in school—a lot of rote learning, great efforts, and a reasonable amount of time have to be invested in memorising these lists, and still, you tend to forget them in a few days. This is when the story method comes to the rescue. In this method, we make a story out of the list given to us using the AIR concept.

ENJOY MAKING STORIES WITH THE STORY METHOD

Making stories is a lot more fun than you think. It is a fascinating and enjoyable process. I will make you understand this with an example.

Memorizing Random Words Using Story Method / Chain Method

- Chocolate
- Mickey Mouse
- Bike
- Car
- Book
- Garden
- Yoga
- Helicopter
- Narendra Modi
- Rahul Gandhi
- Jeep
- Tiger
- Crocodile
- MRI
- Solar Panel

Given above are 15 words unrelated to each other and will take around 15 minutes to memorise by the methods taught in your school. But by training your memory, you can do it faster and retain it for a lifetime. As mentioned in the previous chapter—forget your designations, titles, past experiences, old learning method, and logic and become a kid to learn this method efficiently. Now, let us try to learn these 15 words. To activate your brain and increase concentration—speak out the words loudly.

You can see a pictorial description of those 15 words above. Let us use the story method and with the help of the association, imagination, and ridiculous thinking (AIR) principles, make some sense out of the picture. On the bottom right side of the picture, you can see chocolate in the hand of a mickey mouse sitting on a bike and following a red coloured car. The car is carrying a massive book over which is a beautiful garden where a girl is doing yog exercise. Above the girl, a helicopter is flying, and Mr. Narendra Modi is sitting in it and following Mr. Rahul Gandhi on a jeep. Beside them, a tiger on a tree is watching an ill crocodile undergoing an MRI scan running on solar panels. This is all you need to know. We have made up a story in which every word is associated with one another, imagination principle is used appropriately, and ridiculous thinking is also involved. If you have understood and read the story regarding the image, you will be glad to know that you have memorised those 15 words.

FORWARD

1. ....
2. ....
3. ....
4. ....
5. ....
6. ....
7. ....
8. ....

9. ....
10. ....
11. ....
12. ....
13. ....
14. ....
15. ....

DO SELF-INTROSPECTION

Now, you can test yourself by arranging the words in a forward sequence in the worksheet given below. For example, do you remember that chocolate? Who was holding it? On which vehicle the person was sitting? Whom was he following? What was there above the red car? By asking such questions to yourself, you will be able to arrange all the words in perfect sequence.

Try your hands on reverse sequence. How did MRI work? Who was there in it? Who was watching him? You will be glad that you effortlessly remember the words in reverse fashion as well.

REVERSE

RANDOM WORDS RECOLLECTION

1. ....
2. ....
3. ....
4. ....
5. ....
6. ....
7. ....
8. ....
9. ....
10. ....
11. ....
12. ....
13. ....
14. ....
15. ....

MAKE YOUR STORY PERFECT

You must have noticed that by ridiculously imagining and associating words with one another, you remembered them in a better way. Now I will tell you how to make your story better. For that, you have to remember the word COMB. COMB stands for Colour, Odd, Moving, Big. These are the parameters to make a perfect story. Firstly, you have to add colours to it. Do you know that your brain loves colours? If you are given a choice to watch a black and white movie or a coloured movie, which one will you choose? Coloured one, of course! That is why your story needs to be colourful to make it fascinating. After this, try to make your story—odd, different, or ridiculous so that you can enjoy the process of preparing it. Also, your story must be moving or dynamic—your brain is attracted to things that are in motion. And the last thing is that your story should be big. You must have noticed that you prefer a movie theatre above the TV screen and a TV screen above the mobile screen to watch a movie. It is because your brain finds bigger things better and more understandable. COMB method is something with which you can explore your brain's secrets and create an incredible story. It would help if you tried to utilise maximum senses to make your memory unbeatable. God has given you all these senses so that they can be used properly. The more sense you use, the better your memory will become. You need to see, listen, speak, feel, and indulge yourself completely in this process. In this way, you can drastically improve your memory and life and create a perfect story.

PRACTISE MORE TO LEARN MORE

Now that you know how to make a story and use AIR and COMB methods try attempting these practice sets. I have added two worksheets for you below. You can see some words written on them. Make a story out of them and test yourself by arranging them in forward, reverse, and random sequences. By doing so, you will increase your confidence, memory power, and interest significantly.

First, speak out the given words, then use association, imagination, and ridiculous thinking principles to make a colourful, odd, moving, and big story. Without putting these principles into practise, you won't be able to extract the most out of this book. Hence, it is essential that you honestly do these worksheets for your betterment. Initially, you may face some problems while making stories. But this is a sign that you are improving.You faced problems while learning the English language, driving a car, playing games, or preparing for exams, but you overcame them by consistent efforts. This is what you require here—be consistent, take small steps, and success will be yours. This is no ordinary book; it can change your memory drastically, but only if you do as I say and practise more and more.

Memorizing Random Words Using Story Method /Chain Method

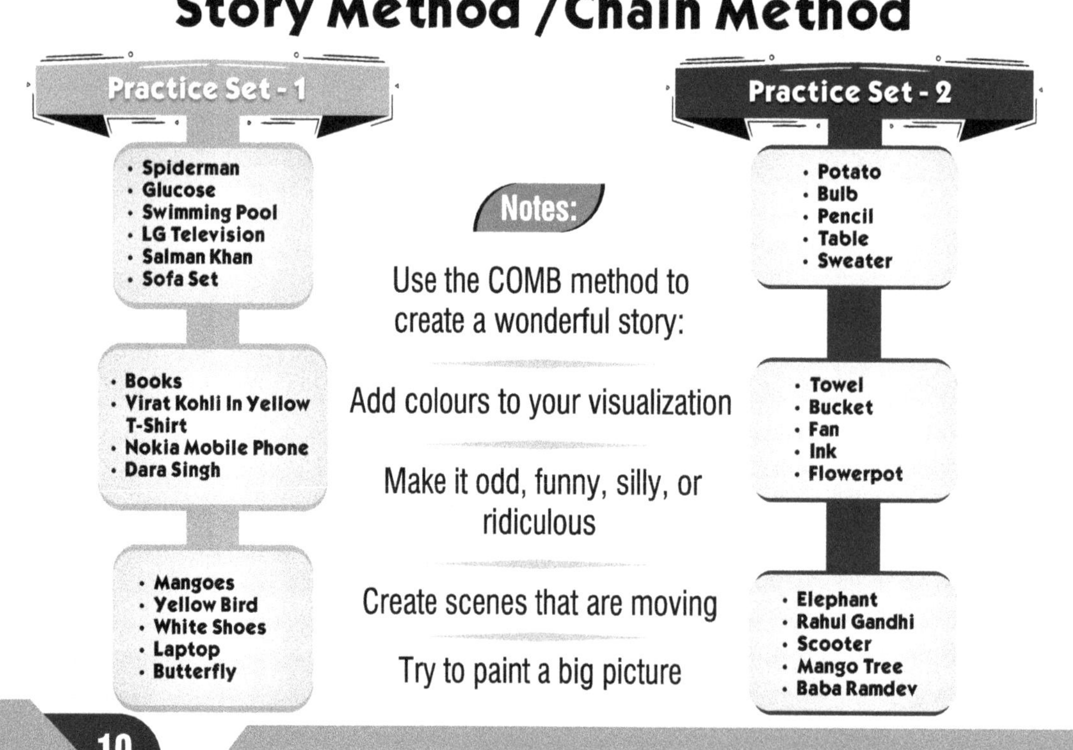

CHAPTER 3

PERFECTLY SHAPE THE MEMORY WITH THE SHAPE METHOD

'Brainpower improves by brain use, just as our bodily strength grows with exercise.'

—A. N. Wilson

Let me tell you about a very useful method called the number-shape method. This method is an advanced version of the story method. With the story method, you could arrange a list of words in forward, reverse, and random sequence by making a story. But there was a limitation in the story method. By using that method, if you were asked to tell the exact position of the item or word in the list, you won't be able to answer. This limitation can be overcome using the number-shape method in which, along with arranging the list of words in forward, reverse, and random sequence, you will be able to remember the exact position of up to twenty items or words. For remembering more than twenty words, I will share a different method. I assure you that the method will be simple, so you don't have to worry about learning new methods, rather enjoy this process like a kid.

RELATE THE SHAPES OF NUMBERS

From the name of this method, you can predict that it will be related to numbers and shapes. Your prediction is correct, as I have told you that your brain works on images and not letters. Therefore, throughout this book, you will learn to convert words and numbers to images to effectively utilise the brain's potential. In this method, you will associate numbers with different shapes and images and ridiculously imagine them. The basis of most of the techniques will be the AIR method.

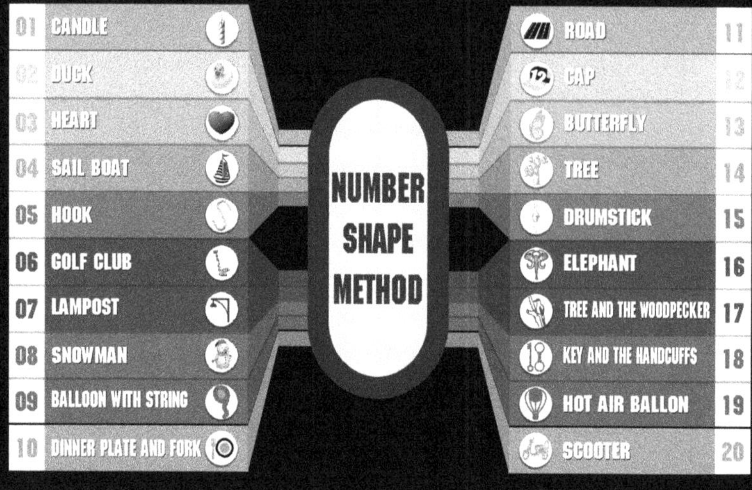

If you are asked, 'With which shape, number one resembles?' What will you answer? Most probably, you will say a candle, stick, or pencil. Right? Various shapes can resemble a single number, but I have chosen the best one out of them for you. So, only twenty shapes or images mentioned in the picture need to be added to your brain right now, and nothing else. Trust me, just by learning the twenty shapes, you will be able to remember uncountable words and lists. Hence, it is worth investing few minutes in memorising these twenty shapes to save hundreds of hours in memorising hundreds of lists.

Now, by referring to the above image, you can say that number one resembles a candle. Similarly, number two resembles a duck. If you take a mirror image of number three, it will somewhat look like a heart. Right? So, you can consider the shape of the number three like that of the heart. You can conclude that number four resembles a sailboat, likewise, five a hook, six a golf club, seven a lamppost, eight a snowman, nine a balloon, and ten a dinner plate with a fork. And, if you look at the shape of number eleven, it will look like a parallel road, similarly, twelve like a cap, thirteen like a butterfly, fourteen like a tree, and fifteen like a drumstick. Like this, sixteen resembles an elephant, seventeen a tree and woodpecker, eighteen a key and handcuff, nineteen a hot air balloon, and finally twenty a scooter.

This is all you need to know to remember any list in any sequence. Now, re-read and master these twenty pairs, and don't move forward until you have learned them. Once you master them, then only you can master their application and implement them.

APPLY THE METHOD CORRECTLY

I hope you have re-read them until they are very clear to you. Now, you are ready to apply this method.

Here, you can see a shopping list, and you are supposed to remember the exact position of the items on the list. With the story method, you can arrange it in forward, reverse, and random fashion, but if I ask you to tell the item in the thirteenth position, you won't be able to answer. Therefore, you will use the number-shape method. Speak out all the words loudly so that your brain can get in attention mode.

In the above image, you can see that I have linked the shapes associated with numbers to the items in the shopping list. For example, do you remember what number one resembled? A candle, right? And the first item on the shopping list was a toothbrush. So, to remember that toothbrush is in the first position, I have associated it with a candle trying to burn it, as it has become useless.

Similarly, I have associated number two, which resembled duck shape with, biscuits, such that the duck is eating the biscuits. In the third position, I have associated honey with a heart that is sweet and pure. In the fourth position, a sailboat is delivering the shampoo that I ordered. At the fifth position, the fresh tomatoes that I bought are hooked so that rats don't eat them. At the sixth position, I replaced the golf stick with a long pen. In the seventh position, because of the streetlight, I am using my phone's torchlight. At the eighth position, an intelligent snowman is buying a notebook to study for IAS exams. At the ninth position, the balloon is putting on sports shoes to lose its fat. And at the tenth position, I have a dinner plate and folk with the help of which I am eating popcorn. So, you see how ridiculously the shape of numbers has been associated with the items on the shopping list. The more funnily linked the images are, the better chances there are to remember them for a longer time.

Furthermore, at the eleventh position, a watch is put on the road to maintain traffic lights. At the twelfth position, a cap is covering the water bottle to stop water leakage. At the thirteenth position, a butterfly is using a yellow highlighter to colour itself. At the fourteenth position, a tree is growing one kilogram of sugar on its branch to add sweetness to its fruits. At the fifteenth position, petrol is filling in a car with a drumstick. At the sixteenth position, the elephant is enjoying eating pizza. At the seventeenth position, the woodpecker is taking a bedsheet for his home. At the eighteenth position, the switch is wearing a handcuff for giving a shock. At the nineteenth position, a photo frame is hanging on a hot air balloon to parcel it to a friend. And finally, at the twentieth position, a cup filled with petrol is put on a scooter.

Now that you have associated all of them try to recall them. For example, what is being burnt with the candle? At what position is that item on the list? What was duck eating? You will be glad to know that you remember the items in the shopping list not only in forward, reverse, and random sequence but also according to their positions.

PRACTISE MORE TO ACHIEVE PERFECTION

It is time to practise what you have learned in this chapter. Here is a list of words where you have to associate the shape of the numbers with the words given in the list.

Try to put them in the correct order in the worksheet below. If you practise sincerely, then you can achieve perfection. Of course, nothing can replace practice; that's why practice as much as possible.

1	11 ....
2	12 ....
3	13 ....
4	14 ....
5	15 ....
6	16 ....
7	17 ....
8	18 ....
9	19 ....
10	20 ....

PRACTICE SHOPPING LIST

Notes:

Number-shape method can be very useful to memorise shopping lists:

- Compare the shape of numbers with similarly shaped objects.
- Associate them with the items in the list.
- Imagine those associations in a funny way

CHAPTER 4

REFINE THE MEMORY WITH THE RHYME METHOD

'Life is about rhythm. We vibrate, our hearts are pumping blood, we are a rhythm machine, that's what we are.'

—*Mickey Hart*

In the previous chapter, you got to know the number-shape method, which was applicable for twenty items. But what if you have to learn forty items? Don't worry. I have the solution for that as well. Using a method called the rhyme method, you can memorise twenty more words from a list. As the name suggests, a rhyming technique will be used to memorise different words. In the previous method, you used shapes to remember the words placed at a specific position. Here you will use rhymes. This method is so easy yet so powerful that it can make you remember items or tasks effortlessly.

RHYME METHOD

1	One	Gun		11	Eleven	Lemon	
2	Two	Shoe		12	Twelve	Shelves	
3	Three	Tree		13	Thirteen	Hurting	
4	Four	Door		14	Fourteen	Mortein	
5	Five	Hive		15	Fifteen	Fitting	
6	Six	Sticks		16	Sixteen	6 Ten	
7	Seven	Heaven		17	Seventeen	Seven Tins	
8	Eight	Skate		18	Eighteen	Waiting	
9	Nine	Wine		19	Nineteen	Namkeen	
10	Ten	Hen		20	Twenty	Plenty	

RHYME TO SHINE

In the above image, you can see that I have listed the rhyming words with each number. Remember to use most of your senses while trying to remember this. Also use the I-factor. Which means while reading the rhyming words, associate themselves with yourself (I) or your experiences. Coming back to the numbers, when you pronounce number one, you can say that it rhymes with gun, bun, or sun. Right? Likewise, two rhymes with shoes, three with a tree, four with door and five with a hive. In this way, number six rhymes with sticks, seven with heaven, eight with skates, nine with wine, and ten with hen. Take a pause and recall what you have read till here. Coming back to the numbers, you can say that eleven rhymes with lemon, twelve with shelves, thirteen with hurting, fourteen with Mortein, fifteen with fitting, sixteen with six-ten, seventeen with seven tins, eighteen with waiting, nineteen with namkeen, and finally twenty with plenty or aunty.

Now, you know which word rhymes with which number. Before moving forward, take a few minutes to revise the rhyme method. Don't forget to imagine and put most of your senses to usewhile reading those words. Use the COMB (Color, Odd, Moving, Big) and AIR (Association Imagination and Ridiculous thinking) methods to remember them for a longer time. If you are given forty items, you can use the rhyme method to remember the first twenty and the number shape method to remember the next twenty items. For instance, if you have to remember the item at the twenty-first position, then ignore twenty and take it as one. And use the number shape method for number one. Similarly, consider the twenty-second position as second and associate the shape of number two with it.

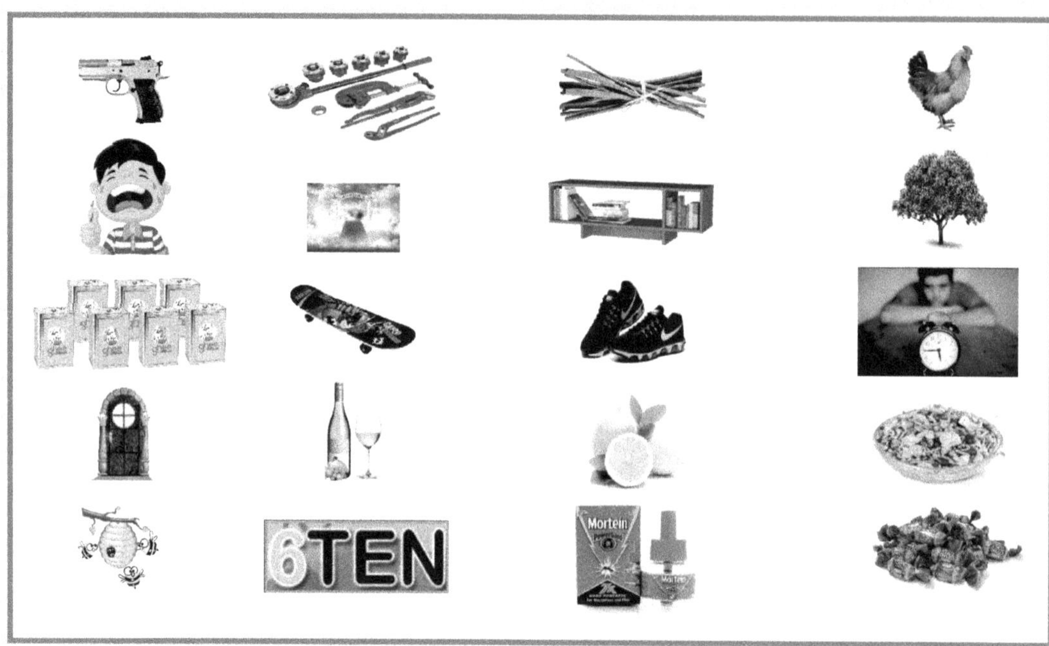

Once you have mastered this, test yourself. Look at the images shown above and write beside them, the number which rhymes with them. The first image is of a gun. Which number from one to twenty rhymes with a gun? You guessed it right. It is number one. Similarly, recall the rest of the numbers by looking at the images.

MEMORISE APPOINTMENTS EASILY

You will be glad to know that you can remember your appointments as well with this rhyme method. And the best part is that you won't require your diary to remember them. Instead, your brain will become your diary.

TRY TO MEMORIZE THESE APPOINTMENTS USING RHYME METHOD

• 7:00am	Morning Walk
• 9:00am	Breakfast
• 12:00pm	Go to Repair Car
• 3:00 pm	Meeting with Amitabh Bachchan
• 5:00pm	To Visit India Gate
• 6:00pm	Go to Coffee Sho

Let's suppose that this is your schedule for tomorrow. As you can see, you have to go for a morning walk at 7 a.m., eat breakfast at 9 a.m., get your car repaired at 12 p.m., and ahem, meet Amitabh Bachchan at 3 p.m. Then you have to visit India Gate at 5 p.m. and go to a coffee shop at 6 p.m. To remember this, I will help you associate the rhyme method with this schedule and funnily imagine them. So please stay in the present and focus here completely to understand it in one go.

7:00 am
Morning Walk

12:00 pm
Go to Repair Car

5:00 pm
To Visit India Gate

9:00 am
Breakfast

3:00 pm
Meeting with
Amitabh Bachchan

6:00 pm
Go to Coffee Shop

So, you are supposed to go for a morning walk at 7 a.m. Right? And the word that rhymes with one is heaven. To remember this, you can say that you will go for a morning walk in heaven. Want to go to heaven? Wait! Don't go so soon. Just go there in your imagination for now. You know, you will realise the need for such associations when you will have something important to do, and you can't afford to forget it. Coming back to your schedule. The rhyming word with nine is wine, and at that time, you have to eat breakfast, so you can remember it by saying that you will take wine with breakfast. Prefer a non-alcoholic, non-harmful wine, of course. Shelves rhyme with twelve, so you can say that you have to repair your car parked on the shelves.

You are aware that tree rhymes with three; therefore, to remember meeting Mr Amitabh at 3 p.m., you can associate the tree with him and say you will meet Mr Amitabh Bachchan under a tree. Hive rhymes with five, and at 5 p.m., you are supposed to go to India Gate. So, you can say that you have to go to India Gate at 5 p.m. to see the biggest hive in the world. As stick rhymes with six, you have to go to the coffee shop at 6 p.m. So, you can say that you will go to a coffee shop at 6 p.m. and stir the coffee with a stick. And you are done with this.

Now, try to recall. What are you supposed to do at 7 a.m.? When do you have to meet Amitabh Bachchan on a tree? When do you have to repair your car parked on shelves? You will eat your breakfast with wine, but when? When will you visit India Gate to watch the biggest hive in the world, and when will you stir your coffee with a stick?If you have paid attention while reading, you would be surprised to know that you remember your schedule in all possible sequences, and if you practise it some more times, you won't have to write your schedule on paper from now onwards.

RHYME METHOD WATCH

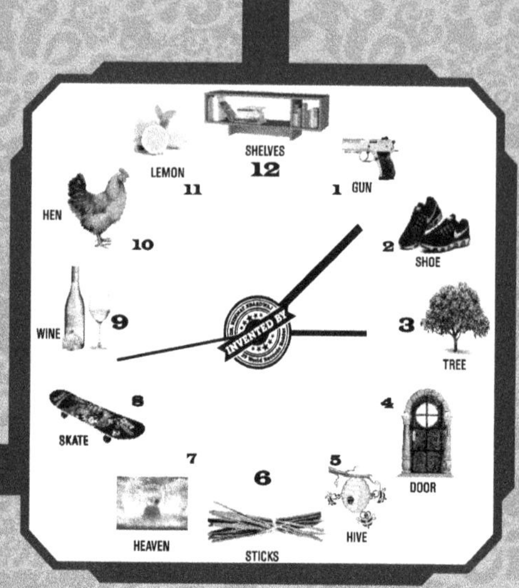

I am concerned about your learning, so I have invented this rhyme method watch to assist you in all ways. With this method, you won't underestimate your brain's potential by writing everything. Rather you will trust your brain to remember them. When you don't use things—they rust. Similarly, when you don't use your memory and brain effectively—they weaken with time. This is the reason why people tend to forget things with time. But I assure you, if you do this memory training sincerely, you will be able to keep your memory as fresh as a daisy. Even when you age, your brain will stay young forever. But for that, you will have to practise. So, make your next day's schedule right now, and using rhyme and AIR methods, try to memorise it.

Notes:

Use the rhyme method to remember words and appointments easily:

- Know the rhyming word with each number.
- Associate that rhyming word with the item or task.
- Make your brain a diary by imagining those associations funnily.

CHAPTER 5

REMEMBER WORDS EFFORTLESSLY WITH THE PNN METHOD

'Nicknames stick to people, and the most ridiculous are the most adhesive.'

—Thomas Chandler Haliburton

Recalling whatever you have studied can be very powerful. That's why I will always recommend you to revise and recall the previous chapters before moving on to a new one. It will take only a few minutes, yet it will impact your performance significantly.

So, till now, you have studied the AIR method—where you were supposed to associate or connect, imagine or visualise, and think ridiculously to remember words or events. As I have said before this method is the foundation of your memory training and will act as a base for almost all memory enhancement techniques. After this, you learnt about the story method—where you created an interesting story out of an unrelated list of words. Then, in the number shape method, you related the numbers with different shapes and then associated them with the words in the list. And then, in the rhyme method, you identified the rhyming words with each number and used the AIR method to link them with a list of items or tasks.

Get the most out of the PNN Method

If you have noticed you applied all these methods on words whose images you knew—your brain already had an image related to them. But what if you are supposed to learn a list of words that are pictureless such as a periodic table, unfamiliar names, places, scientific terms, etc.? It is tougher to remember these things. I agree. That's why I have got a very special method called the PNN or Personal Nick Name method for you. This will solve your problems related to memorisation.

You know you have used this method unknowingly several times by giving personal nicknames to people, places, etc., based on their looks and names—to sometimes ridicule them. This PNN method can be used in various fields. In this method, you will be required to give a personal nickname to the words that you want to remember for a long time. This will be highly useful to memorise technical terms, abstract words, difficult scientific terminologies, names of people, places, inventions, periodic table elements, books and authors, word meanings, etc. As I have told you earlier, your brain requires images to retain information. In the case of the previously mentioned items, there are no particular pictures associated with them in your brain. With this method, you will associate certain pictures with these unfamiliar, unknown, pictureless, and difficult words. To do so, you will have to pronounce the word slowly and divide it into parts to find a familiar, rhyming, or keyword.

IMPLEMENT THE PNN METHOD

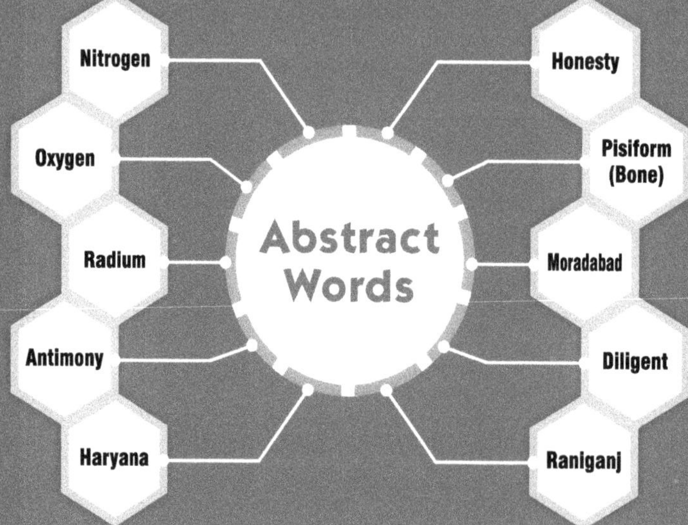

I have learnt all elements of the periodic table, and I have a world record of recalling them in the shortest time. I used this PNN method to make world records, and now I want you to get benefitted from this method.

Coming to the above image, you can see the first word, which is nitrogen. It is a pictureless word, which means that you can't directly make an image of this word in your brain. So, here the PNN method can be used to give a personal nickname to it. Personal nickname means that it can differ from person to person. The nickname that I may create may be different from what you may have in your mind. You should know that your brain needs a trigger to remember things. When you forget some answer during exams, you can recall the whole answer if you get a small clue or trigger. Right? Similarly, this method will provide a trigger for your brain. As Johann Zimmermann says, 'A good name will wear out; a bad one may be turned; a nickname lasts forever.' That's why you will always remember the personal nickname that you have created.

Now, pronounce the first word, i.e., nitrogen. You can relate nitrogen with night. This will act as a trigger for your brain, with which you can recall nitrogen. From oxygen, ox can be remembered. Radium can be associated with radio and antimony with aunty money. Haryana can be related to Harry or the present CM of Haryana, Manohar LalKhattar, or if you are born there, you can use that as a trigger. If you take the middle part of honesty, it will be nest. So, you can remember honesty with the help of nest. While reading these newly associated words, a picture of them will come to your mind, and that's a good sign. Now, what if you have to learn the word pisiform (a type of bone)? You can associate it with a PC form or a form on Personal Computer (PC). From Moradabad, you can connect bad or any other personal nickname that you like. You can associate Delhi intelligent with diligent, and with Raniganj, you can associate rain or rain girl. Now, try to recall each word. Read them aloud and identify their nicknames.

PRACTISE TO STRENGTHEN THE CONCEPTS

Practice Set - 1

1. Vijaywada
2. Nagpur
3. Rajendra Prasad
4. Ukraine
5. Germany
6. Cuba
7. Liberia
8. Japan
9. Grenada
10. Slovakia
11. Helium
12. Potassium
13. Arsenic
14. Cosmic Rays
15. Capacious

The more you practise, the better you will become. So, do two more practice sets. From the above fifteen words, you can conclude that your brain does not have exact pictures for them. Hence, it is difficult to remember them if in case they come as your GK test questions. So, you will associate them with familiar and known words. For example, from Vijaywada, you may be reminded of some Vijay that you know. So, that is how you can remember Vijaywada. Similarly, the nickname for Nagpur can be, nag (snake) pull, Rajendra Prasad— raja praja (king subjects), Ukraine—you crane, Germany—many germs, Cuba—ice cube, Liberia—library, Japan—pan, Grenada—grenade, Slovakia—slow walk, helium—Helen, potassium—pot, Arsenic—nick, cosmic rays—comics, and capacious—cap. So, these were the words and their nicknames. Now, take a pause and see if you remember their nicknames.

1. Chromite	9. Canberra
2. Switzerland	10. China
3. Gujarat	11. Karnataka
4. Amritsar	12. Europe
5. Srilanka	13. Russia
6. Beauty	14. Bihar
7. Africa	15. Punjab
8. Barbados	

In the above practice set, the first word is chromite. The nickname for it can be, crow mic. Similarly, the nickname for Switzerland can be, sweets lands, for Gujarat— gujiya or Mr Modi, Amritsar—Amit Sir, Sri Lanka—Ravan, beauty—Ashwariya Rai or Mother Teresa, Africa—free, Barbados—dosa, Canberra—cobra, China—Xi Jinping or chai (tea), Karnataka— natak (drama) or Taka, Europe—rope, Russia—rusk, Bihar— haar (necklace) or your known person who lives there, and Punjab— bhangra .

I became India's memory king because I have practised a lot and for you to become a memory master, you have to do the same i.e., practise a lot.Slowly with practice, you will be able to use this method everywhere. So have patience and keep practising.

Notes:
Use the PNN method to simplify the memorisation process:
- Create a nickname for a given pictureless word.
- Choose it based on pronunciation, rhythm, or familiar word.
- Use any language that you are comfortable with.

CHAPTER 6

EXPLORE THE SCOPE OF THE PNN AND RHYME METHODS

'The beautiful thing about learning is that nobody can take it away from you.'

—B.B. King

The scope of the rhyme and PNN methods is very vast. To explore them further, first review those methods. In the rhyme method, you linked every number from one to twenty with a corresponding rhyming word. For example, the word that rhymed with one was gun, two was shoes, three was tree, four was door and five was hive. In this way, number six rhymed with sticks, seven with heaven, eight with skates, nine with wine, and ten with hen. Similarly, eleven rhymed with lemon, twelve with shelves, thirteen with hurting, fourteen with Mortein, fifteen with fitting, sixteen with six-ten, seventeen with seven tins, eighteen with waiting, nineteen with namkeen, finally twenty with plenty. And, in the PNN method, you gave personal nicknames to words to make them easier to remember.

MEMORISE GK WITH A TWIST

In competitive exams, it is very common to see GK questions whose answers are pictureless and non-conceptual. One of the familiar topics asked in exams is about Indian presidents. You may know the name of the first president of India—Dr Rajendra Prasad. But do you know the names of second, third, seventh, or eleventh Indian presidents? It's no shock to see such direct questions asked in exams. If you use the general rote learning technique on this, it will be a waste of time, as it will take a lot of time to remember them. Besides this, you won't be able to retain them for a longer time. So, in such circumstances, you can use the rhyme and PNN methods to easily remember them for a lifetime.

List of Indian Presidents

- Rajendra Prasad
- Sarvepalli Radhakrishnan
- Zakir Hussain
- Varahagiri Venkata Giri
- Fakhruddin Ali Ahmed
- Neelam Sanjiva Reddy
- Zail Singh
- Ramaswamy Venkataraman
- Shankar Dayal Sharma
- Kocheril Raman Narayanan
- Avul Pakir Jainulabdeen Abdul Kalam
- Pratibha Patil
- Pranab Mukherjee
- Ram Nath Kovind

RHYME METHOD

No	Word	Rhyme		No	Word	Rhyme	
1	One	Gun		11	Eleven	Lemon	
2	Two	Shoe		12	Twelve	Shelves	
3	Three	Tree		13	Thirteen	Hurting	
4	Four	Door		14	Fourteen	Mortein	
5	Five	Hive		15	Fifteen	Fitting	
6	Six	Sticks		16	Sixteen	6 Ten	
7	Seven	Heaven		17	Seventeen	Seven Tins	
8	Eight	Skate		18	Eighteen	Waiting	
9	Nine	Wine		19	Nineteen	Namkeen	
10	Ten	Hen		20	Twenty	Plenty	

If you are asked to remember these fourteen names for your exams, obviously you will choose to lose marks by not memorising them than trying to learn them. But I don't want that you lose even a single mark. Therefore, I am sharing the tricks to memorise them easily. The first name is Dr Rajendra Prasad. You know, one rhymes with gun. So, you can associate the gun with Dr Rajendra using the AIR method. And, you can say that doctor took out the bullet fired from a huge gun from a patient's body. For the second one, i.e., Mr Sarvepalli Radhakrishnan, you can combine the PNN method and rhyme method. You can give him a nickname like Radha Krishna. And, as two rhymes with shoe—you can say that Lord Krishna gave his shoes to Srimati Radharani so that she can remain protected from thorns on the ground. Don't forget to imagine what you are reading to make a lasting effect on your memory. Next is Mr Zakir Hussain. He can be associated with actor Hussain—who is quite famous because of his shows and ads. You know that three rhymes with tree. So, you can say that Hussain makes his shows under a Peepal tree. In this way, you can remember the exact sequence of each Indian president on the list.

The fourth one is Mr V. V. Giri. His name can be associated with, we Gir. The word that rhymes with four is door. So, you can say that we went into the Gir forest through a door. Fifth is Mr Fakhruddin Ali Ahmed. His nickname can be, Ali. You know that five rhymes with hive. So, you can associate both and say that Ali ran after hitting a hive. Six rhymes with sticks, and you have Mr Neelam Sanjiva Reddy at the sixth position. So, by using the PNN and AIR method, you can say Neelam and Sanjiv fought with sticks. As seven rhymes with heaven and Mr Zail Singh is at the sixth position. Therefore, you can give him a nickname—jail and say that the jail he went to was as pleasant and comforting as heaven. At the eighth position, you have Mr R. Venkataraman. The nickname that you can give to him can be, Venkat Raman. As eight rhymes with skates, you can say that Venkat and Raman bought new skates. As nine rhymes with wine, so for Mr Shankar Dayal Sharma—you can say that Lord Shankar did not recommend wine for anyone. You know that ten rhymes with hen, and to Mr K. R. Narayanan, you can nickname Narayana. In this way, you can say that Lord Narayana opposed eating hens as he created them with love.

As eleven rhymes with lemon, you can say that Dr Kalam used to make delicious lemonade by adding kala namak (black salt). The word that rhymes with twelve is shelves. So, you can say that Mrs Pratibha Patel has a lot of pratibha (ingenuity) to make shelves. Thirteen rhymes with hurting. So, you can say Mr Pranab Mukherjee's mukh (face) hurt after giving a long speech or fighting with opposition parties. Finally, in the fourteenth position, you have Mr Ram Nath Kovind. As fourteen rhymes with Mortein, you can say that Ramu used Mortein to get rid of mosquitos. And you are done! Now, revise these twice to fix them in your brain forever. You will be highly amazed to see the results.

TIME TO TEST YOURSELF

List of Indian Presidents

1	....	8	....
2	....	9	....
3	....	10	....
4	....	11	....
5	....	12	....
6	....	13	....
7	....	14	....

In the above sheet, test your memory and recall all the names according to their sequence. With one and gun, which name did you link? Two rhymes with shoe. Right? So, which name was in the second position? Ask such questions to yourself and fill in the blanks. After filling this, you will get a lot of confidence to face more GK questions as you can now arrange the president list in forward, reverse, or random sequence and tell the exact position of the names in the list. You see, you remember these difficult-to-learn words—this means you have an amazing memory. What you were lacking were just the right guidance and proper memory training. You will get both in this book.

Practise and Boost your Self-Esteem

List of Indian Prime Minister

- Pandit Jawaharlal Nehru
- Gulzarilal Nanda (interim)
- LalBahadur Shastri
- Gulzarilal Nanda
- Indira Gandhi
- Morarji Desai
- Charan Singh
- Rajiv Gandhi
- Vishwa Pratap Singh
- Chandra Shekhar
- P. V Narasimha Rao
- Atal Bihari Vajpayee
- H. D Deve Gowda
- Inder Kumar Gujral
- AtalBihari Vajpayee
- Dr. Manmohan Singh
- Narendra Modi

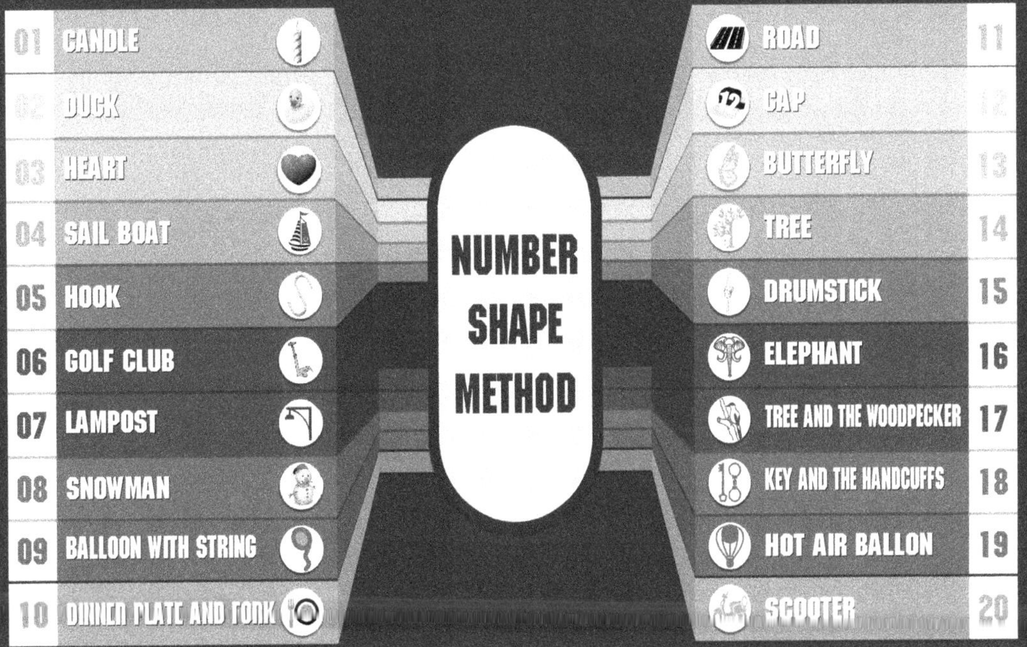

Now try using the number shape and PNN methods on the above list of Indian prime ministers. And, test yourself by filling the names in the worksheet attached below.

List of Indian Prime Minister

1 ....   10 ....

2 ....   11 ....

3 ....   12 ....

4 ....   13 ....

5 ....   14 ....

6 ....   15 ....

7 ....   16 ....

8 ....   17 ....

9 ....   18 ....

Notes:

Previously learnt methods are very effective. They:

- Make memorisation of GK topics hassle-free.
- Have a lot of scopes and can be used widely.
- Make learning fun, easy, and long-lasting.

CHAPTER 7

KNOW THE
DIVERSE APPLICATIONS OF
THE STORY METHOD

'Success is the sum of small efforts, repeated day in and day out.'

—*Robert Collier*

I share specific methods with you only after their proper analysis. I especially take care that the methods that I share are easy to understand and have multiple uses. The story method that I discussed earlier also has various applications. In this chapter, you will get to know the wide scope of the story method. You will learn the names of Indian states and union territories in a different way.

MEMORISE THE LIST OF INDIAN STATES SMOOTHLY

You may be thinking that you remember the names of all Indian states. If this is the case, then take a self-test and try to recall them. Were you able to recall all twenty-eight states? I won't be surprised if your answer is no. Without a proper memorisation technique, it is extremely difficult to remember such a long list of words for a very long time. But if you apply the story method to this, you can learn this easily and that too for a longer period.

MEMORIZING INDIAN STATES

- Andra Pradesh
- Arunachal Pradesh
- Assam
- Bihar
- Chhattisgarh
- Goa
- Gujarat
- Haryana
- Himachal Pradesh
- Jammu and Kashmir
- Jharkhand
- Karnataka
- Kerala
- Madhya Pradesh
- Maharashtra

- Manipur
- Meghalaya
- Mizoram
- Nagaland
- Orissa
- Punjab
- Rajasthan
- Sikkim
- Tamil Nadu
- Telangana
- Tripura
- Uttaranchal
- Uttar Pradesh
- West Bengal

Using the story method, you can make a story out of all these twenty-eight states. But I will initially prefer that you divide these into two parts and make two separate stories. Then, you can make the first story from the list on the left-hand side and the second story from the right-hand side list for your ease.

To start memorising them, first read out the left-hand side list. While you were reading out loud, you must have noticed that these are pictureless words. The last time you used the story method was on words that had some pictures connected to them in your brain like chocolate, mickey mouse, bike, etc. But as this list of words is pictureless—you will have to use the PNN method to give pictures to them, and after that, you can use the story method.

As you can see, Pradesh is common in many states, so you can ignore that and give a nickname to the first part of the state. The first state is Andhra Pradesh. You can give it a nickname— aandhee (storm). The nickname for Arunachal Pradesh can be, Arunima (Indian mountain climber) chal (walk), Assam— aaj shaam (this evening), Bihar—Mr Lalu Prasad (Bihar's famous politician), Chhattisgarh— chattis ghar (thirty-six houses). Goa is quite popular, so you may prefer to not give a special nickname to it. The next state is Gujarat. The nickname you can give to it can be, raat (night). And, the nickname for Haryana can be, Hari ka aana (coming of Lord Hari), Himachal Pradesh— heyy maa chal (o mother let's go), Jharkhand— jharana (waterfall), Karnataka— natak (drama), Kerala— kela (banana), Madhya Pradesh— madhy (middle), and Maharashtra— bada rasta (big path). This completes your first list. You have successfully associated pictures with the names of the states.

CREATE THE FIRST-CLASS STORY

Now, use the AIR method to prepare an amazing story. Along with that, keep imagining and involving most of your senses. You can make a story like this— Aandhee chal rhi hai aur usme Arunima chal rhi hai (Storm is blowing and Arunima is walking in it). Aaj shaam voh Lalu Prasad se milti hai, jinke chattis ghar hai Goa mai (This evening she meets Mr Lalu Prasad who has thirty-six houses in Goa). Jaise hi raat hoti hai Lalu usse ek jagah Bhagwan Hari ke aane ke bare mai batate hai (As the night falls, Lalu tells her about the arrival of Lord Hari at someplace). Darshan ke liye, Arunima apni maa ko sath chalane ke liye kehti hai (For darshan, Arunima asks her mother to go along with her). Unhe raste mai jharna milta hai jaha natak chal rha hota hai (On the way they find a waterfall where a drama is going on). Vaha se voh kele ka prasad lete hai aur Bhagwan Hari ko chadhane ke liye madhy mai ek bade raste par rakh dete hai (From there, they take banana prasad and to offer it to Lord Hari they put it in the middle of a big path).

You can make a personal story and end it in your way. I want to empower you and make you capable. That's why I want you to make a story out of the second list. If I spoon-feed you everything then you won't be able to learn much. So, first, give a personal nickname to each word in the second list then make a story out of them. I will help you by giving hints for nicknames. The nickname that you can give to Manipur can be, money, Meghalaya— megh (clouds), Mizoram— mere (my) Ram, Nagaland—Naga's land, Orissa—Audi, Punjab— punja (claw), Rajasthan— raja ka sthan (king's place), Sikkim— sikke (coins), Tamil— tu mil (you meet), Telangana— tel lagana (apply oil), Tripura— teen (three) puri, Uttaranchal—Aanchal, Uttar Pradesh— uttar (answer), West Bengal—best bangala (bungalow). Now you can easily associate all of them and create a story.

- **Andaman and Nicobar Islands**
- **Chandigarh**
- **Dadar and Nagar Haveli**
- **Daman and Diu**
- **Delhi**
- **Lakshadeep**
- **Pondicherry**

Until you have mastered this method, don't move on to another chapter. Here, a list of union territories is given. Readout loud and give them personal nicknames. After that make a story using the AIR method. Once you are done, don't forget to make a reverse list along with a forward one. Remember, if you write in a reverse sequence, that will benefit you four times more than making a list in a forward sequence. That's why make sure that you prepare a list in reverse sequence and practise well.

Notes:
The story method can help you store a lot of data in memory. It:
- Can be applied to various types of lists.
- Must be complemented with the AIR method and COMB method.
- Should be used after using the PNN method in the case of pictureless words.

MEMORISE DISTRICTS SMARTLY

'The most successful men work smart, not hard.'

—*Bangambiki Habyarimana*

One of my students, Gaurav, made a world record by memorising six hundred districts and recalling them with the highest speed. Inspired by Gaurav, another student asked me if he can also do the same. I replied with a big yes. With my constant motivation and guidance and his smart efforts, he was able to memorise more than six hundred districts. By the way, he is six-year-old. Why am I telling you this? Because if a six-year-old can do it, why can't you? Using the memorisation techniques that I have taught you—you can do miracles and even create world records.

The first principle you should know, to have an amazing memory is association, which means linking or connection. Imagine association as a chain. Just like a chain is formed by joining several links, similarly, an association is formed by joining various words, pictures, or events.

MAKE ANY TASK INTERESTING
Districts of Haryana

- Ambala
- Bhiwani
- Charkhi Dadri
- Faridabad
- Fatehabad
- Gurugram
- Hisar
- Jhajjar
- Jind
- Kaithal
- Karnal

- Kurukshetra
- Mahendragarh
- Nuh
- Palwal
- Panchkula
- Panipat
- Rewari
- Rohtak
- Sirsa
- Sonipat
- Yamunanagar

Here, I will tell you the way to memorise districts by taking the example of Haryana. Initially prefer memorising lists in parts. Consider the left-hand side list to be the first part and the right-hand side list to be the second part. I hope you remember the three-step formula to memorise a pictureless list of words. The first step is to read out loud the names of all the districts. Many names may be new for you, and there may not be any image in your brain related to them. As they are pictureless, so in the second step, you will have to apply the PNN method to give them personal nicknames.

So, the nickname that you can give to Ambala can be, Balaji. And, the nickname that you can give to Bhiwani can be, maa Bhawani, Charkhi Dadri— dadi (grandmother), Faridabad— pari (fairy), Fatehabad—fat, Gurugram—guru, Hisar— hisab (calculation), Jhajjar—judge, Jind— jinn (genie), Kaithal— kitni thali (how many plates), and Karnal— kamal (lotus).

Your third step will be to use the story method to create a story with the help of association, imagination, and ridiculous thinking (AIR) principles. Your story can be like this, Balaji aur maa Bhawani ke mandir mai dadi jo ki ab fat pari ban gayi hai, guru jo ki judge ban gaye hai aur jinn hisab kar rahe hai ki kitni thali aur kamal mandir se gayab ho gaye hai (In Balaji and mother Bhawani's temple, a grandmother who has now become a fat fairy, a guru who has become a judge, and genie are calculating how many plates and lotuses have disappeared from the temple).

Now, try to work on the second list. Complete the three steps religiously to get the best outcome. First, read out the list. Second, give a PNN to each one of them. Kurukshetra is quite famous because of Mahabharat and Bhagavad Gita. So, you may not give a special nickname to it. The nickname for Mahendragarh can be, Mahindra, Nuh—no, Palwal— parmal (a kind of vegetable), Panchkula— paanch kulla (five times gargles), Panipat— pani puri (golgappe), Rewari— rewadi (a food item), Rohtak—road tak (till), Sirsa—sir, Sonipat— sona (gold), and Yamunanagar—Yamuna.

The third step is to make a story. For that, you can refer to this story, Kurukshetra mai Mahindra no karta hai parmal khane ke liye aur paanch kulle karke pani puri aur rewari khane road par chala jata hai. Vaha usse uske sir milte hai jo sona lene Yamuna paar karke aaye hai (In Kurukshetra, Mahindra says no to eat parmal and after five times gargles, he goes to a road to eat golgappe and rewadi. There, he meets his sir who has come to take gold after crossing Yamuna).

And it's done. Congratulations! Now recall the two stories. I am sure if you have read it carefully, personalised it, and involved your senses, you must have remembered most of it. If not, don't worry. Just keep trying. Practice makes a man perfect. These methods awaken your interest, activate your dormant brain, increase your focus and bring out your creative self. At least these are much better than rote learning where to remember lists; you would have to repeat it twenty or thirty times.

Let me give you a challenge—memorise the names of the districts of your state. Use the three-step formula, i.e., speak it out, use the PNN method, then make a story using the story method. I am sure you will take this challenge with a high josh and complete it before moving on to the next chapter.

Notes:
Memorising districts is easy:
- Read out the names.
- Give each of them a personal nickname.
- Create a story out of them.

CHAPTER 9

LEARN PERIODIC TABLE IN A SIMPLER WAY

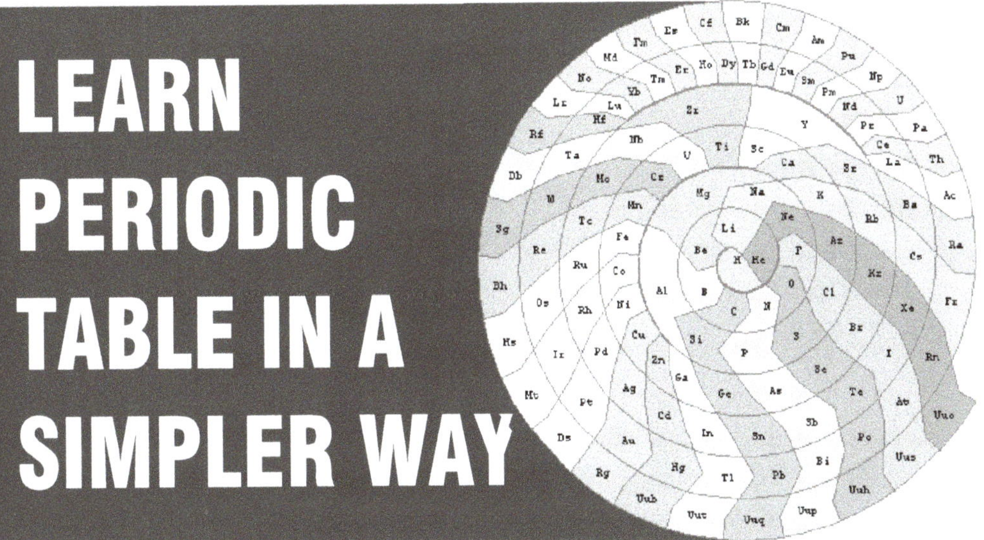

'What the ocean was to the child, the Periodic Table is to the chemist.'

—*Karl Barry Sharpless*

I know what students feel when they are asked to learn the periodic table. It is one of the most tiring and boring tasks to memorise if done by rote learning. As the periodic table is a common topic for school and competitive exams, so it can't be ignored—it needs to be faced. If this is the case, why not face it happily and make it interesting?

When I memorised and recalled the entire periodic table, it became a headline in various newspapers. My students also learnt it and got featured in newspapers. I don't have a background in chemistry, yet I made a world record by recollecting all the 118 elements of the periodic table in just 21.62 seconds. The chemistry students and teachers I met don't remember the complete table even after studying it for years. But my five-year-old student remembers it. Why? Because of the methods that I have taught him. You can also memorise all of them by practice and smart work.

GET PERIODIC TABLE AT YOUR FINGER-TIPS

- **Hydrogen**
- **Helium**
- **Lithium**
- **Beryllium**
- **Boron**
- **Carbon**
- **Nitrogen**
- **Oxygen**

- **Fluorine**
- **Neon**
- **Sodium**
- **Magnesium**
- **Aluminum**
- **Silicon**
- **Phosphorus**

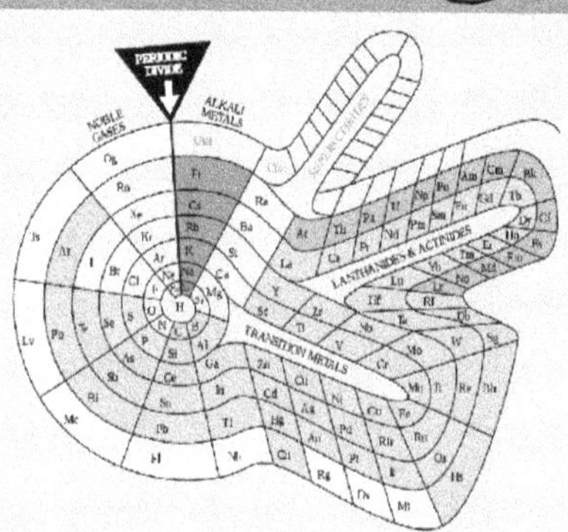

Right now, I have shared fifteen elements with you. There are118 elements, so you can make approximately seven or eight stories to learn the complete periodic table. And, by spending one hour per day—you can memorise it completely in a week. Moreover, once you have done this, you can retain it for a lifetime. So, it is a win-win situation.

First, recite or read out loud all the names. As you can observe, all of them are pictureless. But you know that your brain requires images to remember stuff. So, what will you do? Yes! You will associate images with them using the PNN method. In the second step give personal nicknames to all words. This second step is crucial, so don't skip it or go directly to the story method. The nicknames you can give to hydrogen can be, balloon (hydrogen-filled), helium—Helen, lithium—litchi, beryllium—berry, boron— bori (sack), carbon—car, nitrogen—night, oxygen—ox. And for other second list, the nicknames can be like, fluorine—floor Rin (soap), neon—knee, sodium—soda, magnesium—Maggi, aluminium— aloo (potato), silicon—cone, phosphorous—horse.

In the third step, make a story using the AIR method. And the story can be like this— Ek hydrogen se bhare balloon mai Helen beth kar litchi kha rahi hai. Berry ke ped se takrane ke baad Helen bori par gir jati hai aur car lekar night mai ox ke sath ghar jati hai. Ghar mai uski maa rin se floor saaf kar rahi hai. Helen geele farsh par gir jati hai aur uski knee par chot lag jati hai. Galti se voh dawai ki jagah, soda laga leti hai, jis vajah se dard badh jata hai. Fir uski maa uske liye special Maggi banati hai uske favorite aloo dalkar ek cone ki shape mai, jis se usme horse jaisi power aa jati hai. (In a hydrogen-filled balloon, Helen is sitting and eating litchi. After hitting a berry tree, Helen falls on a sack and takes the car to the house with an ox. At home, her mother is cleaning the floor with soap. Helen falls on the wet floor and hurts her ankle. By mistake, instead of medicine, she puts soda, due to which pain increases. Then her mother makes a special Maggi for her by adding her favourite potato in the shape of a cone, which gives her horse-like power).

TAKE EXTRA STEPS TO GET EXTRA BENEFITS

Now try to recall the elements from this story. For example, which element you associated with the balloon and Helen? What are you reminded of when you hear Maggi? Likewise, recollect otherel ements in both forward and reverse sequence. After this, apply the three-step formula on the list given below and try to memorise them.

Periodic Table

- **Sulphur**
- **Chlorine**
- **Argon**
- **Potassium**
- **Calcium**
- **Scandium**
- **Titanium**
- **Vanadium**
- **Chromium**
- **Manganese**
- **Iron**
- **Cobalt**
- **Nickel**
- **Copper**
- **Zinc**

Notes:
The periodic table is not difficult to learn:
- Divide all the elements into seven or eight parts.
- Give each of them a personal nickname.
- Make an interesting story out of each part.

CHAPTER 10

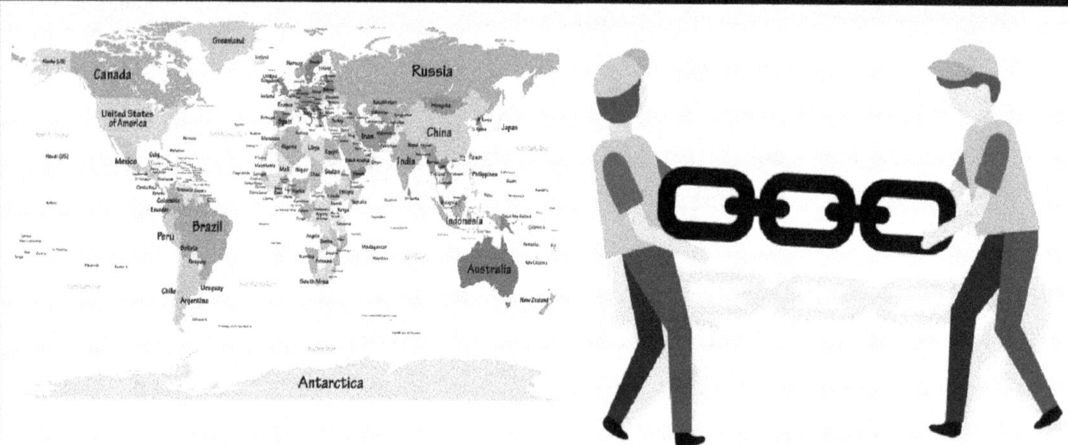

'A step towards what you fear is a step towards mastering it.'

—Matshona Dhliwayo

ountries and capitals can be comfortably memorised using a certain method. I have made a world record in this category. Also, many of my students have memorised all countries and their capitals, currencies, parliament, etc. It is not rocket science. With proper techniques and training, you can do it too. The method that will help you a lot in this process is the link method. It is a very simple yet highly useful method to memorise GK facts. This is the secret formula behind the success of many people. The link method is a sub-set of the story method. In the story method, a story is usually made after associating many words with one another. Whereas in the link method, a link or short story is created between two words.

CREATE FASCINATING LINKS TO MAKE LEARNING EXCITING

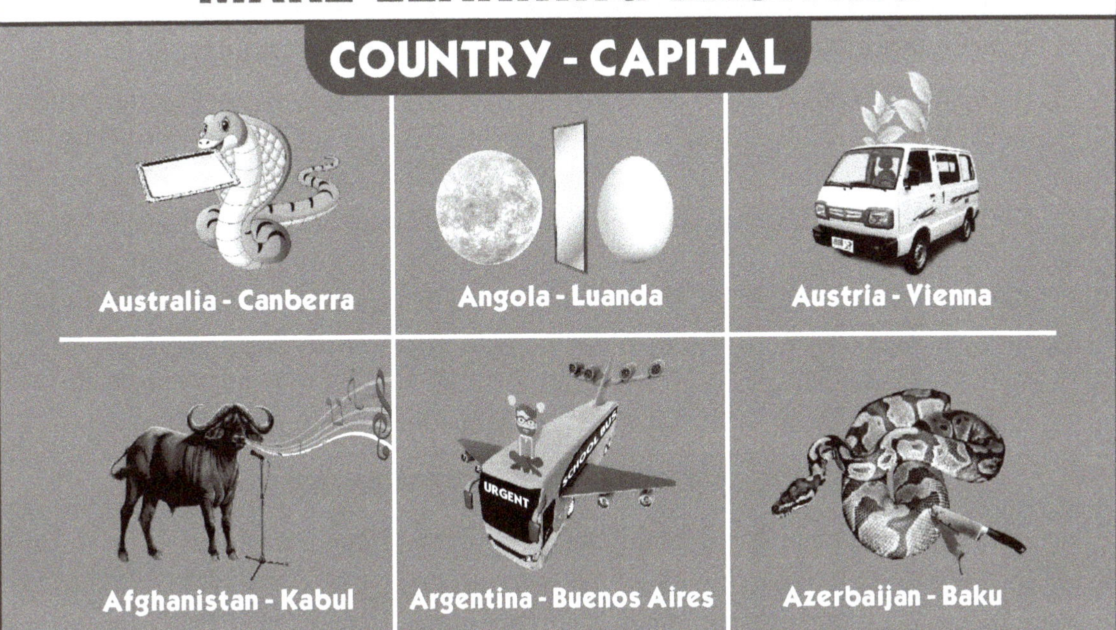

Do you know questions based on countries and their capitals are among the favourites for competitive exam paper setters? Therefore, it becomes necessary to learn them.To make this learning process easier for you,I have shared some pictures above, where countries and their capitals have been linked together using the link method. You will have to use the same three-step method to memorise them. Just remember that in the third step, instead of making one long story for all words, you will have to make links or short stories for each pair of country and its capital. Use the AIR method, and don't forget to make it colourful, odd, moving, and big (COMB). Remember to involve your senses—read, speak, hear, feel, and visualise properly. Indulge yourself completely in this process of learning and exploring new things.

First, read out the words. As these are pictureless words, so you will have to give them personal nicknames using the PNN method. Here, the given nicknames are for your reference. You can create your personal nicknames based on your experiences and imagination. After giving them nicknames, you can link them easily. The nickname you can give to Australia can be, tray liya (bring), and the nickname for its capital, Canberra can be, cobra. The link or short story for this pair can be, cobra muh mai tray liya aa raha hai (a cobra is coming with a tray in its mouth). The nickname for Angola can be, aag ka gola (fireball) and for Luanda, it can be, anda (egg). The short story for this pair can be, aag ka gola sheeshe mai dekhane par anda jaisa lag raha hai (a fireball is looking like an egg while viewing in a mirror). The nicknames for Austria can be, oss (dew) and Vienna—van. So, they can be linked by saying, van ke upar paudha ug raha hai aur uss par oss gir rahi hai (a plant is growing on the top of a van, and dew is falling on it). The nicknames for Afghanistan and Kabul can be, gaane ka sthaan (place of singing) and bull respectively. And, they can be linked as bull gaana ga raha hai gaane ke sthaan par (a bull is singing at the place of singing). The nicknames for Argentina and Buenos Aires can be, urgent and bus air respectively. They can be linked by a short story—due to urgent work I am travelling by bus that flies in the air. The nickname for Azerbaijan can be, ajagar bejaan (lifeless python) and for Baku, it can be, chaku (knife). The short story associated with them can be, voh ajagar ko chaku se bejaan kar rahe hai, jo dusro ko khane vala tha (they are killing a python with a knife, who was about to eat others).

This method may not make sense to some, but trust me, many people have made records with this method. It is a very student-friendly and effective method.

PUSH YOUR LIMITS AND ATTEMPT MORE

COUNTRIES & THEIR CAPITAL

COUNTRY	CAPITAL	COUNTRY	CAPITAL
Australia	Canberra	Bhutan	Thimphu
Afghanistan	Kabul	Brazil	Brasilia
Angola	Luanda	Cameroon	Yaounde
Argentina	Buenos Aires	Chile	Santiago
Austria	Vienna	Canada	Ottawa
Azerbaijan	Baku	Colombia	Bogota
Bangladesh	Dhaka	Comoros	Moroni
Barbados	Bridgetown	Costa Rica	San Jose
Belgium	Brussels	Cuba	Havana
Bulgaria	Sofia	Cyprus	Nicosia
		Dominica	Roseau

You must have got a good idea of using this method to smoothly memorise countries and their capital. As you can see in the above image, you have covered till Azerbaijan and Baku. Likewise, try to attempt the rest of them. First, read them out, then give them personal nicknames, and finally link the countries to their capitals.

The nickname for Bangladesh can be, bangla (bungalow) and Dhaka can be, dhakaah (push). The link in-between them can be created by saying, voh bangle ko dhakaah de rahe hai dusri jagah le jane ke liye (they are pushing the bungalow to move to another place). Barbados can be associated with bar bar dosa (again and again dosa) and Bridgetown with bridge. They both can be linked together by saying, voh bar bar dosa kha raha hai bridge par bethkar (he is eating dosa again and again while sitting on the bridge). The nickname for Belgium can be, gym and Brussels can be, Bruce Lee. They can be linked by saying, Bruce Lee is continuously dancing in the gym. The nicknames for Bulgaria and Sofia can be, bull gira (fell) and sofa, respectively. Their short story can be, uske sapne mai bull gir raha hai uske sofa par (a bull is falling on his sofa in his dream).

Coming to the next column, the nickname for Bhutan can be, bhoot (ghost), Thimphu—tempo, Brazil— jheel (lake), and Brasilia— asli le aa (bring real). And, the short stories for these two pairs can be, jis tempo mai voh betha hai, usse bhoot chala raha hai (a ghost is driving the tempo in which he is sitting) and voh mujhe keh raha hai ek bada jheel asli ka le aa (he is telling me to bring a real lake). The nickname that you can give to Cameroon can be, camera room, Yaoundé— gunde (goons), Chile—chilly, and Santiago—aunty go. Each pair can be linked by these two short stories— room ke camera se pata chala ki vaha gunde aa rahe hai (a camera in the room showed that the goons are coming) and aunty go, bring chilies for me. The nickname for Canada can be taken as candy, Ottawa—auto (rickshaw), Colombia—call lambi (long), and Bogota— baag (garden). The short stories after linking them can be, he is selling candies on rickshaw to sustain his family and inti lambi call chal rahi hai ki baag ke sau chakar lag jayenge (there is such a long call going on that a hundred rounds of garden will be covered). The nickname for Comoros can be, rusk, Moroni— mor (peacock), Costa Rica—cost rack, and San Jose—Sam josh (zeal). They can be linked by saying, mor ko uske favourite rusk khila rahe hai dher sare log (a lot of people are feeding the peacock with its favourite rusk) and Sam josh mai aakar sabse mehnge rack ka cost puch raha hai, ab usse voh khareedna hi padega (Sam is excitedly asking the cost of the most expensive rack, now he has to buy it). The personal nickname for Cuba can be, cube, Havana— havan (a fire ritual), Cyprus—Sai, and Nicosia— nikat (near). You can link each pair by saying, voh ice cube daal rahe hai havan mai (they are putting ice cubes in havan) and Sai hamesha nikat rehte hai sabke (Sai always remain close to everyone).

Finally, the nicknames for the last pair, Dominica and Roseau can be, Dominos and rose, respectively. They can be linked by saying, Dominos is starting new pizza made up of roses.

Congratulations! With this, you have memorised around twenty-one pairs of countries and their capitals. Instead of the usual and boring rote method,you chose the interesting and creative method to learn them.

COUNTRIES & THEIR CAPITAL

COUNTRY	CAPITAL	COUNTRY	CAPITAL
Denmark	Copenhagen	Hungary	Budapest
Ecuador	Quito	India	New Delhi
Estonia	Tallinn	Iran	Tehran
Ethiopia	Addis Ababa	Japan	Tokyo
Fiji	Suva	Norway	Oslo
Finland	Helsinki	Portugal	Lisbon
France	Paris	New Zealand	Wellington
Germany	Berlin	Samoa	Apia
Greece	Athens	Pakistan	Islamabad
Grenada	Saint George's		

Now, challenge yourself and memorise these above-mentioned countries and their capitals using the link method. After this, try to learn the names of all the countries and their capitals of the world. If not all, learn at least all the famous countries and their capitals. Keep involving most of your senses in this process, and don't forget to enjoy this journey. You can achieve the extraordinary. I have full faith in you.

Notes:

Countries and their capitals can be comfortably learnt using the link method:
- Read out their names loudly.
- Give a personal nickname to each one of them.
- Link two words together and make a short story.

CHAPTER 11

GET COUNTRIES AND THEIR CURRENCIES AT YOUR FINGER-TIPS

'Once you have mastered the craft, you can use it for whatever purpose you choose.'

—Hassan Fathy

I hope you have practised countries and their capitals. Now, take one step forward and learn about countries and their currencies using the very simple link method. In competitive exams, it is common to see countries and currencies related problems. Do you remember what you have to use while trying to memorise them? Yes! Your senses. And? AIR and COMB methods. See, your memory has already improved.

LINK COUNTRY WITH ITS CURRENCY EASILY

Here, some of the countries and their currencies are given. Memorise them using the three-step formula. First, read out the names of all the words given above. Then give a personal, familiar, and suitable nickname to each word. And, finally, create a link between the nicknames of the country and its capital. Try to keep the nicknames for countries the same as in the last chapter.

The currency of Indonesia is Rupiah. The nickname you can give to Indonesia can be, inn dono ne (both of them) Siya and Rupiah's nickname can be, rupaya (rupees, Indian currency). So, the story after linking them can be, inn dono ne mata Siya ko rupaya lautaya (Both of them returned the money to goddess Siya). The nickname for Austria and its currency, euro can be, oss (dew) and hero, respectively. The short story from this can be, hero Amitabh Bachchan ke hath mai paudha hai jispar oss giri hui hai (hero Amitabh Bachchan has a sapling in his hand on which dew has fallen). Bermuda's nickname can be, var muda (groom turned) and dollar's nickname can be, doll. So, they can be linked by saying, var muda doll se shadi karte samay (groom turned while marrying the doll). Italy's nickname can be, idli and euro's nickname can be, hero, as defined earlier. The link that joins them can be, hero Rajnikanth ate idli for hours. The nickname for Botswana and Pula can be, boat rawana (left) and pull (bridge). Their short story can be, voh paani mai kudh gaya aur boat rawana kar di pull ke niche se (he jumped into the water and left the boat under the bridge). The nickname for Brazil can be, badi jheel (big lake), and its currency, real can be associated with Real (fruit juice company). In this way, they can be linked by saying, yeh badi jheel Real fruit juice se bani hui hai (this big lake is made up of Real fruit juice). Now, take a pause and recall them.

KEEP it Up, Do Some MORE

COUNTRIES & THEIR CURRENCIES

COUNTRY	CURRENCY	COUNTRY	CURRENCY
Australia	Dollar	Indonesia	Rupiah
America	Dollar	Italy	Euro
Albania	Lek	Austria	Euro
Armenia	Dram	Botswana	Pula
Bahrain	Dinar	Bermuda	Dollar
Bulgaria	Lev	Brazil	Real
Canada	Dollar	Haiti	Gourde
France	Euro	Somalia	Shilling
Ghana	Cedi	Yugoslavia	Dinar
Japan	Yen	Mongolia	Tugrik

Now, memorise the currencies of the countries given above. What are you supposed to do first? Yes, recite their names. Read them out loud. The first pair is of Australia and dollar. The nicknames for them can be, tray liya (bring tray) and doll, respectively. They can be linked by saying, usne kaha doll se ki tray liya (he told doll to bring a tray). The nickname for America can be, Donald Trump (45th U.S. president) and dollar's nickname can be, doll, as usual. So, their short story can be, Donald Trump married a beautiful doll. The nicknames for Albania and Lek can be, all banned and lake, respectively. They can be linked by saying, ducks banned all people from coming into the lake. The nickname for Armenia can be, army, dram—drum, Bahrain—bahar (outside) rain, dinar—dinner, Bulgaria—bull gira (fell), and lev—leaf. The short story for Armenia and dram can be, army officers are playing drums on the heads of enemies. The link between the nicknames of Bahrain and dinar can be, unhone bahar rain ke pani se dinner banaya (they made dinner from outside rainwater). The nicknames of Bulgaria and lev can be, linked by saying, bull gira, leaf se takrane ke baad(the bull feel, after hitting the leaf). Remember, you have to make ridiculous or funny connections. So that your brain can retain them for a longer time. The nickname that you can give to Canada can be, candy, dollar—doll, France—dance, euro—hero, Ghana—khana (food/dinner), cedi—CD, Japan—jaa (go) paan, and yen—yeh (this). The stories that can be made from the nicknames of Canada and dollar, and France and euro can be, doll ate the candy at midnight and hero danced with her in her dreams. The short stories that can be made from the nicknames of Ghana and cedi, Japan, and yen can be, unhone khane mai CD khaya tha (they ate CD for dinner) and usne mujhe kaha jaa paan le aa, yeh jo ad mai dikhaya tha (he told me to get a pan that was shown in the ads).

Coming to the next column, you can notice that you have already covered till Brazil and real. So, start by giving nicknames to Haiti and gourde. Their nicknames can be, hathi (elephant) and guard. Their one-liner story can be, yaha hathi ko guard ki tarah istamal kiya jata hai (here elephant is used as a guard). Somania's nickname can be, so (sleep) money and shilling's nickname can be, chill. A link can be created between them by saying, usko sone aur chill karne ke money milte hai (he gets money to sleep and chill). The personal nickname that you can give to Yugoslavia can be, you go slow, dinar—dinner, Mongolia—manga liya (ordered), and tugrik—tanga. Their short stories can be, you should go slow as you ate dinner just now and maine tanga mangaya Ola app se ghar jane ke liye (I ordered tanga from Ola app to go home).

Save Parliaments' Names Permanently in your Memory

COUNTRIES & THEIR PARLIAMENTS

COUNTRY	PARLIAMENT	COUNTRY	PARLIAMENT
America (U.S.A)	Senate	Denmark	Folketing
Afghanistan	Shora	Germany	Bundestag
Albania	People's Assembly	Hungary	National Assembly
Andorra	General Council	India	Sansad
Britain	Parliament	Iran	Majilis
Bulgaria	National Assembly	Japan	Diet
Brazil	National Congress	Norway	Storting
Canada	Parliament	Portugal	Assembly of the Republic
Colombia	Congress		
Egypt	People's Assembly	New Zealand	Parliament
Dominica	House of Assembley	Samoa	Fono
		Pakistan	Senate

Now that you have covered some important currencies, try to memorise countries and their parliaments using the link method. Once you are done with this, then you can confidently say that you have capitals, currencies, and parliaments at your finger-tips. You know what most people don't. You are training your memory well. Congratulations!

Notes:

Countries and their currencies can be learnt using the link method:

- Read out their names.
- Give a personalised nickname.
- Use the link method to link the pair.

CHAPTER 12

RETAIN MINERALS AND THEIR ORIGIN FOR A LIFETIME

You just have to have the guidance to lead you in the direction until you can do it yourself.

—*Tina Yothers*

I have been in the memory field for more than thirteen years. So, I am aware of the needs of students and professions. That's why out of the hundreds of methods, I select a few highly useful methods for you that can be applied in many different areas.

The methods you have learnt till now are very powerful and useful. They have various applications. With the story method, you can make your learning process fun. Using the PNN method, you can turn all unfamiliar words in the world into familiar ones. And by using the link method, you can link two words very easily. You have memorised countries and their capitals and currencies. Now, you will memorise minerals and their place of origin in a very interesting and convenient manner.

TRY TO MEMORIZE THESE MINERALS AND THEIR PLACES USING PNN METHOD

Minerals	Source/Places
Gypsum	Rajasthan
Gold	Hatti
Diamond	Chhatapur
Chromite	South Africa, Canada, Finland, and Madagascar
Oil	Digboi
Bauxite	Kerala
Gold	Kolar

Remember that there is no need to give nicknames to words that are known to you, and your brain already have images associated with them. To memorise the given list, first of all, read out all the words. After that, use the PNN method to make the words familiar. Then, finally, link the pair by making a one-liner story.

The first pair is gypsum and Rajasthan. Gypsum's nickname can be, Gypsy and Rajasthan's nickname can be, raja ka sthan (king's place). They can be linked by saying, raja ke sthan mai rani Gypsy chalati hai (the queen drives a Gypsy in king's place). As gold, diamond, and oil are familiar minerals, so there is no need to give special nicknames to them. The nickname that you can give to Hatti can be, hathi (elephant). Gold and Hatti's nickname can be linked by saying, vaha hathi gold se bane hote hai (there, the elephants are made up of gold). Chhatarpur's nickname can be, chaata (umbrella). Diamond and Chhatarpur nickname's one-liner story can be, bina barish ke bhi voh diamond ka chaata istamal karta hai (he uses a diamond umbrella even without rain). The nickname for chromite and Cuttack can be, crow mic and kaatata (cut), respectively. They can be linked by saying, crow mic par gaate hue usse kaatata hai (the crow bites the mic while singing). The nickname for Digboi can be, dog boy. Oil and Digboi nickname's one-liner story can be, dog applies oil on a boy's hair. Bauxite's nickname can be, boxer and Kerala's nickname can be karela (bitter gourd). Their one-liner story can be, boxer din mai teen baar karela khaala hai fit rehana ke liye (boxer eats bitter gourd three times a day to stay fit). The nickname for Kolar can be, collar. Gold and Kolar's nickname can be linked by saying, he wears a shirt with a collar made up of gold.

Now, try to recall all of them. What was the nickname that you gave to gypsum? Where is it found? With which word did you associate Hatti? In which two places gold is commonly found? Take a self-test and answers such questions.

Expand your Memory and Learn More

TRY TO MEMORIZE THESE MINERALS AND THEIR PLACES USING PNN METHOD

Minerals	Source/Places
Brass	Moradabad
Coal	Raniganj
Cement	Katni
Steel	Rourkela
Petrochemicals	Koyali
Mica	Jharkhand
Cotton	Nagpur

You are given some more minerals and their place of origin. Read out the names loudly. You will notice that coal, cement, steel, and cotton are familiar words. So, you don't have to give specific nicknames to them. For the rest of the words, you can use the PNN method to give nicknames.

Brass' nickname can be, grass and Moradabad's nickname can be, mor (peacock). Their one-liner story can be, grass par mor nachata aur gata hai (peacock sings and dances on grass). Raniganj's nickname can be, rani (queen). Coal and Raniganj's nickname can be linked by using the link method. Their one-liner story can be, coal par rani chalati hai (queen walks on coal). Katni's nickname can be, chutney. The one-liner story for cement and Katni's nickname can be, voh cement se chutney banata hai (he makes chutney from cement). The nickname for Rourkela can be, kela (banana). Steel and Rourkela's nickname can be associated by saying, voh steel se bana kela khata hai (he eats banana made of steel). The nicknames for petrochemicals and Koyali can be, petrol and koyal (cuckoo), respectively. Their one-liner story can be, koyal petrol bharti hai gadi mai (a cuckoo fills petrol in a car). Mica's nickname can be, mic and Jharkhand's nickname can be, jharna (waterfall). Their one-liner story can be, voh jharne ke andar mic par gaata hai (he sings with a mic inside the waterfall). Nagpur's nickname can be, nag (snake). Cotton and Nagpur's nickname can be linked by saying, voh cotton se bane nag se logo ko darata hai (he scares people with a snake made up of cotton). That's it.

Do you know apart from your memory, one more thing is improving? Your general knowledge! Yes, this book will not only act as a memory enhancement book but also a general knowledge improvement book. By sincerely following what is being taught here, you will get a perfect combination of a good memory and great general knowledge. Just keep practising and strengthening your concepts. Trust me, you have a lot of potentials. Don't underestimate yourself and your memory.

Notes:
Minerals and their place of origins can be remembered for a lifetime:
- Read out the names.
- Use the PNN method.
- Link each pair of minerals to their sources.

CHAPTER 13

Remember Inventors and their Inventions

Easily

'Every beginner possesses a great potential to be an expert in his or her chosen field.'

—*Lailah Gifty Akita*

You must have experienced that you forget crucial information during exam time. But with a trigger, you can instantly remember that data. Mere rote learning can't help you to get a trigger. But the methods that you have learnt in this book will help you, for sure. They will provide you with triggers that will guide you when you want to recall the information. In this chapter, you will learn how to memorise the names of inventors and their inventions easily. By learning them using the link method, you will be able to create lifelong triggers in your brain.

Learn Everything Easily with the Right Strategy

INVENTORS - INVENTIONS

Graham Bell - Telephone

Marconi - Radio

Madam Marie Curie - Radium

Galileo - Telescope

James Watt - Steam Engine

J.L. Baird - Television

Firstly, read out all the names. Secondly, use the PNN method. And finally, link the inventor with his invention. You will notice that most of the inventions' pictures are there in your brain, i.e., you are already familiar with them. So, you don't have to give a special nickname to them. Also, don't forget to use the COMB and AIR methods. Along with that, keep involving your senses and use the I-factor while giving nicknames to words and linking them to another word. Stay active and enjoy this process.

The nickname for Graham bell can be, garam bail (hot bull). So, telephone and Graham bell's nickname can be linked by saying, garam bail ke sar par rakha hua telephone jal gaya (the telephone kept on the head of the hot bull burnt). Mr Marconi's nickname can be, maar kohni (hit elbow). The one-liner story that can be made from Marconi's nickname and his invention, radio can be, usne mujhe kaha maar kohni radio par tabhi chalega yeh (he told me to hit elbow on the radio only then it will work). Madam Marie Curie's PNN can be, madam marry and radium's nickname can be, ready. They can be linked by saying, madam is ready to marry sir. Galileo's nickname can be, galee (lane). His nickname can be linked to his invention, telescope by saying, galee mai bohot bada tolooopo aaman se tapka hai (a big telescope has fallen from the sky in the lane). The nickname for James Watt can be, jam wait. His nickname can be linked to his invention, steam engine by using the link method. Their one-liner story can be, jam could not wait to meet bread, so it travelled on a steam engine to reach bread's home. J. L. Baird's nickname can be, jail bird. His nickname can be linked to his invention, television by saying, in a television show, a bird is kept in jail as it stole food.

Now, try to recall what you have learnt. What did Graham Bell (garam bail) invent? What was Marconi's (maar kohni) invention? Ask such questions to yourself and keep revising until you have memorised them.

TRY TO MEMORIZE THESE INVENTIONS AND THEIR INVENTORS USING PNN METHOD

Inventor / Discoverer	Invention / Discovery
C V Raman	Raman Effect
Robert Wiliiam Thomson	Rubber Tyre
Elisa Otis	Lift
Fahrenheit	Thermometer
Bush well	Submarine
J.J Thomson	Electron
Samuel Morse	Telegraph
Christopher Sholes	Type writer

Read out the names loudly. Now before linking them, give them nicknames. C. V. Raman's discovery of the Raman effect can be easily remembered by their common word, i.e., Raman. Robert William Thomson's nickname can be, robot. His nickname can be linked to his invention, rubber tyre by saying, robot converted itself into a rubber tyre. Remember, you have to make the associations ridiculously so that your brain can retain that. Elisa Otis's nickname can be, Nisha notice. Her nickname and invention, lift can be linked by saying, Nisha notices the lift every day for many hours. You know that temperature in a thermometer is calculated in terms of Fahrenheit. So, that can act as a trigger for you to remember the invention of Fahrenheit, i.e., thermometer. Bush Well's nickname can be, Bruce Lee. His nickname and invention, submarine can be linked by saying, Bruce Lee fights with the enemy submarine every day. J. J. Thomson's nickname can be, Thom's son and electron's nickname can be, election. They can be linked by saying, Thom's son voted for the opposite party in the elections. The nicknames for Samuel and telegraph can be, mor (peacock) and graph, respectively. Their one-liner story can be, mor uska graph banata hai (a peacock makes his graph). Christopher Sholes' nickname can be, Krish topper. His nickname and invention, typewriter can be linked by saying, Krish is a topper, still he got an old typewriter as a prize. And you are done.

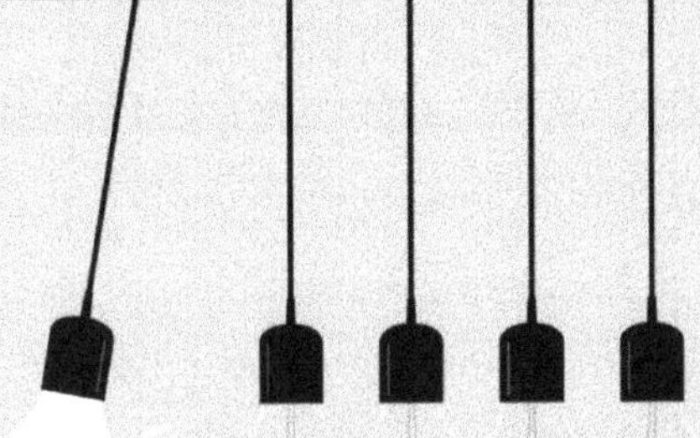

FROM ORDINARY TO EXTRAORDINARY

When I was in my first year of college, one of my classmates brought a file containing many newspapers and magazines' cuttings. The media coverages were of his inventions that he invented. He brought that to impress the professors. When I asked him to show the file to me, he refused and continued showing it only to professors and people whom he thought were worthy of looking at his achievements. At that moment, I realised how good a person would feel when his name appears in the news, how proud the parents of that inventor must be, and how amazing it is to keep a file full of pictures of oneself with one's inventions and accomplishments. With that burning desire to contribute something to the world, make my parents proud, and see my name in the newspaper, I did hard work smartly.

A time came when almost all newspapers published my achievements in the fields of Vedic maths and memory. Google search engine is filled with my media coverages. Now, I don't just have one file to show but many files. I have been covered more than five hundred times by the media. Even when I leave this world, my name and discoveries will stay here forever and will be of some use to people.

I first memorised a five thousand years calendar, then one lakh and finally unlimited years calendar. Then I put in all my knowledge to create a one-page secret calendar which contained everything a person needs to know to tell the exact date of any year. This gave me the title of inventor. I got featured again and again in many famous English and Hindi newspapers and news shows. I have shared this secret calendar with all my students because I want everyone to improve and succeed. I don't want to hide any study or memory improvement secrets from my students. I made several world and national records and also created a complete memory and math lab. I don't share my accomplishments with you to show off. I share them to ensure you that you are in safe hands. You are learning from an expert who has a lot of experience in this field. Trusting your guide is a crucial part in this journey of learning. Also, I keep telling you about myself to boost your confidence and inspire you. If I can do it, coming from a humble background, then you can definitely do it. You can do miracles. You can be extraordinary.

Notes:
The study of inventors and their inventions can be made interesting:
- Read out all the given words.
- Give nicknames to unknown or pictureless words.
- Use the link method and associate the inventor with his invention.

CHAPTER 14

Memorise Important Details Related to Countries

Comfortably

'You can't build a great building on a weak foundation.'

—*Gordon B. Hinckley*

You have already learnt the names of countries and their capitals, countries and their currencies. But what if you have to learn the names of countries and their capitals, currencies, and continents altogether? How will you proceed? Yes! You will use the link method. By using it, you will create a short story to memorise all the information. If the items in the list increase further, then you can gradually increase the length of the story by keeping the methods and techniques the same. Don't worry, I will guide you throughout the process. Before proceeding with the main topic, I would like to remind you of some basic yet crucial things. To master the memory, you need constant revisions. In the urge to move forward you should not forget the foundational things.

Make your Foundation
UNSHAKABLE

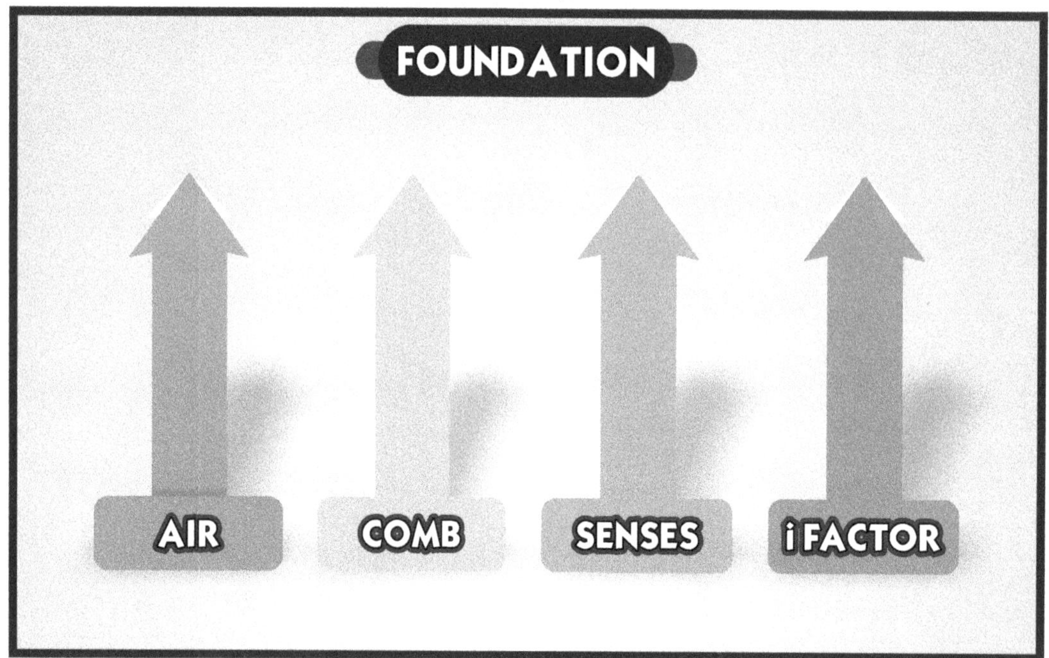

To reach great heights, your foundation needs to be very strong. And, the foundation of this entire book lies in these four things mentioned in the above image. The association, imagination, and ridiculous thinking principles helps you memorise things more interestingly and effectively. The COMB principle reminds you that your story needs to be colourful, odd, moving, and big. Involving senses during the entire process of memorisation helps the brain to remember information for an extended period. And, the I-factor personalises the learning process. In this, you associate the given data with yourself and your experiences. This makes the information personal and helps you to immerse yourself (I) in this completely.

Along with all these, emotions play a critical role. Extreme emotional events leave a permanent mark on your brain. If I ask you, 'What did you do in the last weekend?' You may not be able to answer. But if I ask you, 'What did you do on your birthday or some special day?' You will be able to recall quickly. This is the magic of emotions. When we attach emotions to information, we are more likely to remember them. Hence, keep using the AIR and COMB methods and utilise your senses, I-factor, and emotions as much as possible.

Memorise Difficult Things

Without Difficulty

Country, Capital, Currency & Continent

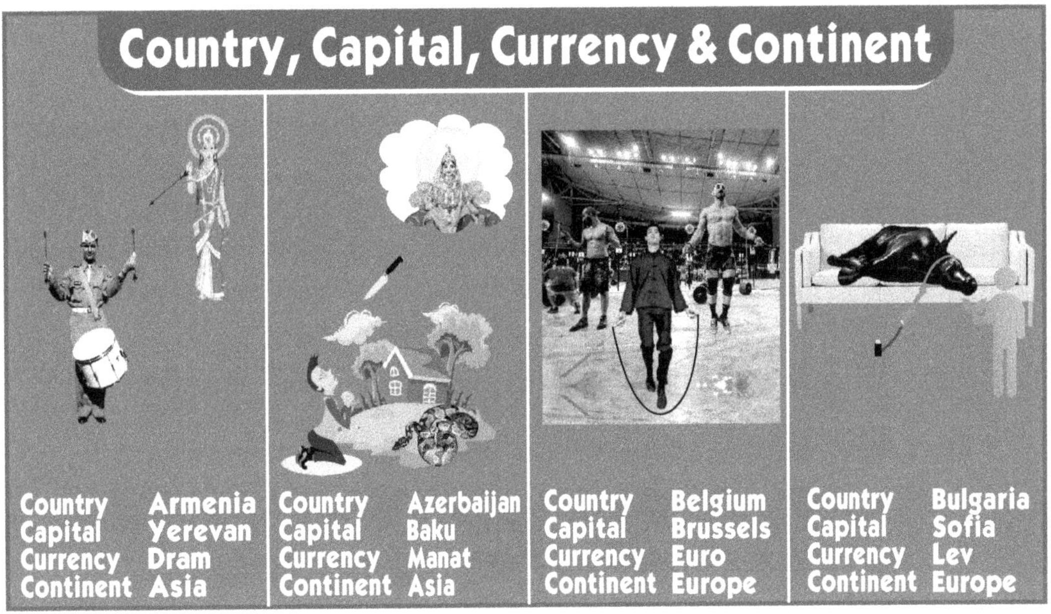

Proceed step by step. In step one, read out all the names. In step two, associate the pictureless words with some pictures. And in step three, link them together by making a short story using the link method.

I hope you have read the names properly. Now, you can see that the first country is Armenia. Its nickname can be, army. Its capital, Yerevan's nickname can be, yeh le baan (take this arrow). Its currency, dram's nickname can be, drum. And, its continent, Asia's nickname can be, Siya (Goddess Sita). So, the short story that you can create by linking these four words can be, mata Siya ne army man ko baan dia drum bajane ke liye (Goddess Siya gave arrows to army man to play drums). The next country is Azerbaijan. Its nickname can be, ajgar bajjan (lifeless python). Its capital, Baku's nickname can be, chaku (knife). Its currency, manat's nickname can be, mannat (vow). And, its continent, Asia's nickname can be, Siya. So, by linking all of them your story can be somewhat like this, chaku marne se baijan hue ajgar ko dekh kar, maine mannat mangi mata Siya se ki usse theek kar den (seeing the lifeless python killed by a knife, I made a vow to Goddess Siya to revive him). For Belgium, the personal nickname can be, jinn (genie). Its capital, Brussels' nickname can be, Bruce Lee. Its currency, euro's nickname can be, yaaro (friends). And, its continent, Europe's nickname can be, rope. After linking these four nicknames, the short story can be, gym mai Bruce Lee apne yaaro ke saath rope jumping kar raha hai (in the gym Bruce Lee is jumping rope with his friends). The last country is Bulgaria. Its nickname can be, bull gir gaya (bull fell). Its capital, Sofia's nickname can be, sofa. Its currency, lev's nickname can be, leaves. And, its continent, Europe's nickname can be, rope. You can link all these by creating a short story like, jab bull gir gaya sofa par toh usne usse rope se bandh kar leaves khilaya (when the bull fell on the sofa, then he tied it with a rope and fed it with leaves).

Now, revise all that you have learnt. Once you have revised, then recall the information. For example, what is the capital, currency, and continent of Armenia (army)? What is Azerbaijan's (ajgar baijan) capital? Without peeking at the solutions, try to answer more such questions. The more you practise, the better your results will be. These simple methods will help you a lot in exams. Instead, not only in exams but also in all other areas of life such as relations, career, extra-curricular, etc. I accept that initially, it will take some time and effort, but eventually, I can guarantee—you will become an expert in this area. And, this will make you and your memory extraordinary.

Below, I have attached two practice sets for you. Memorise them using the PNN and link method. Ideally, you should not move to the next chapter without completing them. So, take your time and memorise them sincerely.

Practice Set - 1

	Country	Capital	Currency	Continent
1	Afghanistan	Kabul	Afghani	Asia
2	Albania	Tirane	Lek	Europe
3	Algeria	Algiers	Dinar	Africa
4	Andorra	Andorra la Vella	Euro	Europe
5	Angola	Luanda	New Kwanza	Africa
6	Antigua & Barbuda	Saint John's	East Caribbean dollar	North America
7	Argentina	Buenos Aires	Peso	South America

Practice Set - 2

	Country	Capital	Currency	Continent
8	Armenia	Yerevan	Dram	Asia
9	Australia	Canberra	Australian dollar	Oceania
10	Austria	Vienna	Euro	Europe
11	Azerbaijan	Baku	Manat	Asia
12	The Bahamas	Nassau	Bahamian dollar	North America
13	Bahrain	Manama	Bahrain dinar	Asia
14	Bangladesh	Dhaka	Taka	Asia
15	Barbados	Bridgetown	Barbados dollar	North America

Notes:

Nothing is difficult to memorise once you know the basics:

- Use the basic AIR and COMB methods.
- Keep involving your senses, I-factor, and emotions.
- Utilise the PNN and link methods to memorise data related to countries.

CHAPTER 15

Store Books and their Authors in Memory *Forever*

'The swiftest way to triple your success is to double your investment in personal development.'

—Robin Sharma

Books and authors are among the favourite topics of the examiners. I have got many messages and emails asking how to remember the complicated names of books and authors. When I shared these methods with those students, they were able to memorise the names very quickly. They were astonished by the results, and you will be too. Your experience of memorising the names of inventors and their inventions will be helpful herein learning the names of books and their authors.

Never Forget these Prime Methods

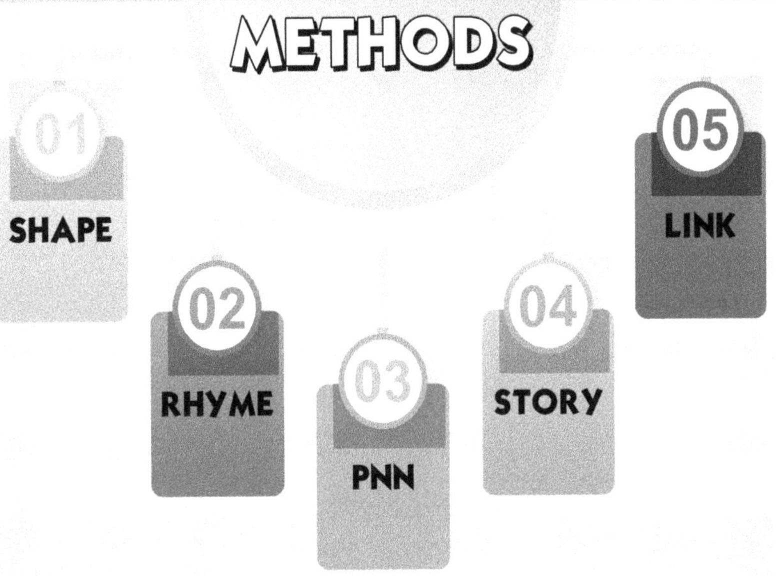

Before moving forward with the books and authors, briefly revise the methods you have studied. If the principles that you revised in the previous chapter are considered as a road then these methods are the vehicles to reach your destination. Therefore, it is essential to keep them in mind. In the shape method, you associated shapes of the number with some images and used them to remember lists of words. In the rhyme method, you found out the word that rhymes with each number and then used it appropriately. In the PNN method, you gave pictures to pictureless, unknown, or unfamiliar words. This helped you to remember the words easily. In the story method, you made a story out of some given words by implementing the AIR and COMB methods. The link method is a sub-set of the story method. In that, you linked the given words to make an exciting and ridiculous one-liner (very short) story. These methods are highly useful and important. Therefore, keep using them in the required places to get a stronghold over them.

Memorise Books and Authors Like

Never Before

BOOKS & AUTHORS

	BOOK	AUTHOR
1	A Tale of a Tub	Jonathan Swift
2	Madhushala	Harivansh Rai Bachchan
3	Godan	Prem Chand
4	Anand Math	Bankim Chandra Chatterjee
5	Gitanjali	Rabindra Nath Tagore
6	My Experience with Truth	Mahatma Gandhi
7	Discovery of India	Pandit Jawaharlal Nehru
8	Babarnama	Babar
9	Wings of Fire	Dr. A.P.J. Abdul Kalam
10	Arth Shastra	Kautilya
11	The God of small Things	Arundhati Roy
12	Room on the Roof	Ruskin Bond

Start by reading out all the names in a sequence. Use the PNN method, then the link method. Remember, there is no need to give special nicknames to books or authors you are familiar with. So, the first book is A tale of a Tub. Its nickname can be, tel (oil) tub. Its author, Jonathon Swift's nickname can be, Swift (Maruti Swift car). After associating these two ridiculously, you can make a short story somewhat like this, tub mai tel bhara tha toh usne ussi se apni Swift car dho di (the tub was filled with oil so he washed his Swift car with it). Don't forget to imagine while making associations and reading these one-liner stories. Imagination or visualization is a crucial part of memorisation.

The next book is Madhushala. Later, I will share how one line from this book motivated me throughout my journey. Madhushala's nickname can be, madhu (honey) and its author, Harivansh Rai Bachchan's nickname can be, Amitabh Bachchan. They can be linked by saying, Amitabh Bachchan madhu se nahate hai

(Amitabh Bachchan takes a bath with honey). Godan's nickname can be, gau daan (cow donation). Its nickname and author, Prem Chand's name can be linked by saying, usne prem se chand ko gau dan kar di (he donated a cow to the moon with love). Keep imagining all of these to store them in your permanent memory. Anand Math can be remembered from Anand's name, who started the Super 30 concept. So, its nickname can be, Anand maths. Its author, Bankim Chandra Chatterjee's nickname can be, banking chand (moon). Their one-liner ridiculous story can be, Anand sir maths padhate hai banking students ko chand par (Anand sir teaches maths to banking students on the moon).

The next book is Gitanjali. Its nickname can be, Gita Anjali. Its nickname and author, Rabindranath Tagore's name can be linked by saying, Rabindranath gave lessons on Gita to Anjali. My Experiments with Truth is a quite famous book. It is an autobiography of Mahatma Gandhi. So, their one-liner story can be, Mahatma Gandhi came to my home to share his experiments. Jawahar Lal Nehru wrote Discovery of India book. It can be memorised by saying, Jawahar Lal discovered India. The next book is Akbarnama. Its nickname can be, Akbar naam (name). Its author, Abul Fazl's nickname can be, bull fasal (crop). Their short story can be, bull fasal par Akbar ka naam likh raha hai (the bull is writing Akbar's name on crop). I hope you remember that you can create your own story as you like.

Wings of Fire is a book written by Abdul Kalam. They can be memorised by linking in this way, Abdul Kalam being a Scientist invented wings made up of fire. Kautilya who is famously called Chanakya, wrote Arthashastra book. Arthashastra's nickname can be, earth shastra (scriptures). This can be memorised by making a one-liner story. It can be like, Kautilya learnt all the shastras there on Earth. The God of Small Things is a book written by Arundhati Roy. The author's nickname can be, Arun ro (cry). So, their one-liner story can be, Arun rota hai God se small things mangane ke liye (Arun cries for asking small things from God). Room on the Roof is a book by Ruskin Bond. Ruskin Bond's nickname can be, rusk band (close). So, the author's nickname and book's name can be linked by saying roof vale room ko band krke voh rusk kha raha tha (he was eating rusk by closing the room on the roof). And, you are done with the given list of books and their authors.

As I said earlier, I want to share my favourite line from the book Madhushala, which has always inspired me. It is, raah pakad tu ek chala chal, paa jaega madhushala (pick a path and keep walking, you will find the tavern). Roughly thirteen years ago, I developed an interest in the memory and maths world. But I lacked resources, parental support, books, mentors, role model, and knowledge of career options in this field. I knew even if I tell someone about my dream, they won't support me rather they will criticise. So, I hid my desire from all. The line, raah pakad tu ek chala chal, paa jaega madhushala kept motivating me to take steps towards my goal. I spent whatever small amount of pocket money I had—in a cybercafe to learn memorisation techniques and methods. I did not tell anyone for three to four years and kept working on my goal. Every day I improved myself and worked on my weak areas. Then a time came when not I but newspaper told my success story. I made a world record and became famous across the nation. After seeing this, my parents accepted my choice.

If I would have feared about the future, stopped in between, and did not take any step to improve, then I would not have reached here. I followed my passion, raah pakadi aur chalta gaya (took the path and went on). With time my fame increased but there was still no source of income. My parents started raising this point related to earning. Then I again reminded myself of, raah pakad tu ek chala chal, paa jaega madhushala. I did not lose hope, trusted my ability, and took steps to transform things. And with time, from the field which was unheard of by anyone, I started to earn a lot. And I still make an excellent amount of money from this field. I love doing this.

By telling you all this, I wanted to emphasise that you can do anything, if you are determined to do it. Even God comes to help that person. With faith in God and yourself, you can achieve anything. If there is something that you are passionate about, but the world won't understand or accept then keep working on your passion without telling the world. Let your success make the noise. Invest time on that every day and do it secretly for some time. Raah pakad tu ek chala chal. You may not get support initially, but everyone will start supporting you when you achieve success in your choice of field. Don't let the expectations and criticisms of the world slow you down. I believe in you. You can do it.

Notes:
Books and their authors are no longer hard to learn:
- Read out the names in sequence.
- Give personalised nicknames to unfamiliar names.
- Use the link method to link books with their author.

CHAPTER 16

'If you're walking down the right path and you're willing to keep walking, eventually you'll make progress'

—Barack Obama

I deliberately chose states and their capital topic because students tend to forget and ignore the smaller yet crucial topics. It is important for all to know the names of states and their capitals not just because it is a common topic for exams but because as a responsible citizen of India you should know the basic details of your country. It is an embarrassing moment when someone asks about the capital of a famous state and you are not able to tell. It has happened to me in my childhood, that's why I don't want you to face the same situation.

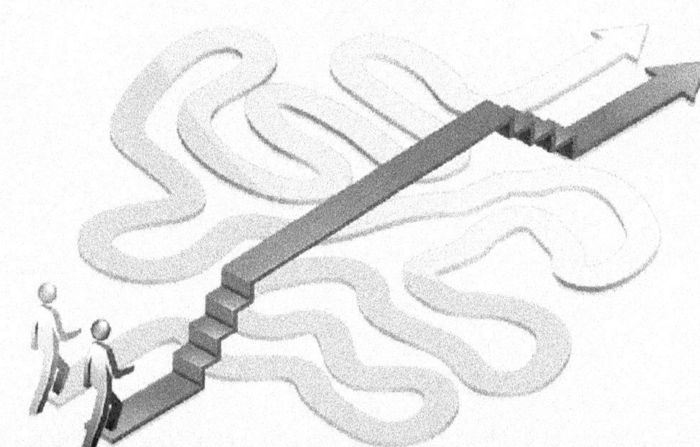

Shortcut Ways to Learn States and their Capitals

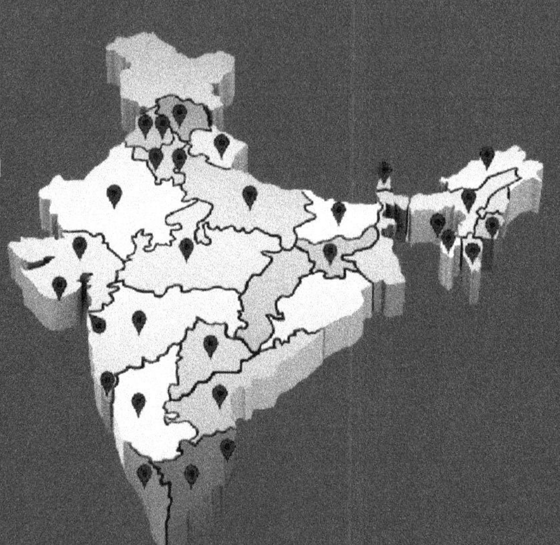

I am sure you know what you have to do. Yes! Proceed with the three-step formula. Read out all the names. Give nicknames to unfamiliar or challenging words, then link the pair together. First, one is Andhra Pradesh. Its nickname can be, aandhi (storm). Its capital, Hyderabad's nickname can be, hara baag (green garden). Their short story can be, mera hara baag aandhi aane se kala pad gaya (my green garden turned black due to the storm). Arunachal Pradesh's nickname can be, Arunima chal (walk). Its capital, Itanagar's nickname can be, eet nagar (brick town). So, you can say that, Arunima tez chal rahi hai eet se bane nagar samay par pahuchane ke liye (Arunima is walking fast to reach the town made of bricks on time). Next is Assam. Its nickname can be, aaj shaam (this evening). Its capital, Dispur's nickname can be, disc. You can combine them by saying, pure shaher ne aaj shaam disc jane se mana kar diya (the whole city refused to go to the disc this evening). Bihar can be related to its ex-CM, Lalu Prasad. And, its capital, Patna can be associated with Tina. Their short story can be, Lalu Prasad and Tina Dabi studied together for the Civil Services exam. The next state is Chhattisgarh. Its nickname can be, chattis ghar (thirty-six houses). Its capital, Raipur's nickname can be, ripe. Their one-liner story can be, chattis gharo ke sabhi phal ab ripe ho gaye hai (all the fruits of thirty-six houses are ripe now). Goa's nickname can be, go. Panaji's nickname can be, PUBG. They can be linked by saying, I dreamt that my father happily permitted me to go and play PUBG. The next state is Gujarat. Its nickname can be, gujari raat (spent night). Its capital, Gandhinagar's nickname can be, Mahatma Gandhi. Their one-liner story can be, maine raat gujari Mahatma Gandhi ke sath (I spent the night with Mahatma Gandhi). Lastly, Haryana's nickname can be, Hari ka aana (coming of Lord Hari) and its capital, Chandigarh's nickname can be chand ghar (moon house). Their short story can be like, aaj bhagwan Hari ka aana hua mere chand jaise ghar mai (today Lord Hari has come to my moon like house).

Achieve Perfection with Perfect Practice

STATES & THEIR CAPITALS

STATE	CAPITAL	STATE	CAPITAL
Himachal Pradesh	Shimla	Punjab	Chandigarh
Jharkhand	Ranchi	Rajasthan	Jaipur
Karnataka	Bengaluru	Sikkim	Gangtok
Kerala	Thiruvananthapuram	Tamil Nadu	Chennai
Madhya Pradesh	Bhopal	Telangana	Hyderabad
Maharashtra	Mumbai	Tripura	Agartala
Manipur	Imphal	Uttar Pradesh	Lucknow
Meghalaya	Shillong	Uttarakhand	Dehradun
Mizoram	Aizaw	West Bengal	Kolkata
INagaland	Kohima		
Odisha	Bhubaneswar		

As you have understood the concept, now try to memorise these states using the same methods. I can easily tell you the nicknames and stories of these. But it won't serve the purpose of this book. I want you to progress. And in this journey of learning, self-study plays a vital role. Only with practice and self-study you can master your memory and GK. Of course, your mind will trick you and tell you to skip this and move on to another chapter. But you should take charge of your mind and thoughts and align them in the direction of success and not procrastination.

PERMANENTLY MEMORISE
Rivers and their Places of Origin

Rivers and their Places of Origin

River	Places of Origin
Ganga	Gangotri (Uttarakhand)
Yamuna	Yamunotri (Uttarakhand)
Indus	Mansarovar (Tibet)
Narmada	Maikal Hills, Amarkantak (MP)
Tapi/Tapti	Satpura Range, Betul (MP)

I hope you have read out all the names. The first river's name is Ganga, and its place of origin is Gangotri. They can be easily remembered by associating Ganga with Gangotri. You can clearly see the presence of the name Ganga in Gangotri, so it is easy to memorise. Likewise, the place of origin of Yamuna, i.e., Yamunotri can be easily remembered because of the common word Yamuna. Next is Indus. Its place of origin is Mansarovar. Mansarovar's nickname can be, man and Indus' nickname can be, das (ten). They can be linked together by saying, uss man ke das sar hai (that man has ten heads). Narmada's place of origin is Maikal Hills. Narmada's nickname can be, nar maada (male female). Maikal Hills' nickname can be, Michael hil (shake). Their one-liner story can be, Michael hil gaya itne sare nar maada ko dekh kar (Michael was shaken to see so many males and females). Last is Tapi. Its nickname can be, paapi (sinner). Its place of origin, Satpura Hills' nickname can be, satya hil (truth shake). Their short story can be, voh paapi ka satya sunkar sab hil gaye (everyone was shaken to hear the truth of that sinner).

Rivers and their Places of Origin

River	Places of Origin	River	Places of Origin
Mahanadi	Nagri Town (Chhattisgarh)	Sabarmati	Udaipur, Aravalli Hills (Raj.)
Brahmaputra	Chemayungdung (Tibet)	Ravi	Chamba (Himachal Pradesh)
Sutlej	Mt Kailash (Tibet)	Pennar	Nandi Hills, Chickballapur (Karnataka)
Beas	Rohtang Pass (H. Pradesh)		
Godavari	Nasik (Maharashtra)	Luni	Pushkar, Aravalli Hills (Raj.)
Krishna	Mahabaleshwar (Maharashtra)	Chambal	Janapav, Indore, Vindhyas (MP)
Cauvery	Brahmagiri Hills, Coorg (Karnataka)	Teesta	Cholamu Lake (Sikkim)
		Rangeet	Rathong Glacier (Sikkim)

Now, it is time to practise. Memorise the given names and prove your potential. These techniques and methods have the capacity to change your life. But only when you implement them. Mere theory won't give you results.Therefore, you have to apply your knowledge.

Notes:

The link and PNN methods have a lot of applications:

- States and their capitals can be memorised smartly.
- Rivers and their places of origin can be remembered for a lifetime.
- Many different types of lists can be learnt in a short time.

CHAPTER 17

Get

MASTERY

OVER NUMBERS BY USING THE PHONETIC METHOD

'Number rules the universe.'

—*Pythagoras*

Have you faced difficulty learning dates of historical events; latitude and other numerical facts in geography; boiling points, atomic numbers, weights in chemistry; numerical constant values in physics; phone numbers of people; birth dates of friends; ATM pins; account numbers; etc.? No need to worry now. You won't face these problems again. The method that I will be sharing here is life-changing. With this method, you can easily memorise everything where digits are involved. This will help you not only in your studies but also in your daily routine. This method is called the phonetic method. As you know, your brain requires images to remember things efficiently, but digits are pictureless. So, it is difficult to remember them.

WITH PHONETIC METHOD

Suppose you are given this sentence to remember, 'I love memorising things using these methods and techniques.' This is a fifty-one-lettered sentence that you can remember easily. But if I give you fifty-one-digit number like, '8965 6785 6789 2314 5427 6789 4563 5678 3098 6710 4580 1023 890'. Will you be able to memorise this? I know it does not seem possible. But with the phonetic method, it is possible.

I gained a lot of popularity by applying this method in real life. When I was called for TV shows or newspaper interviews, I was asked to recall a hundred-digit number, sometimes a five-hundred-digit number, and once I was given a one-thousand-digit number to recall on the spot. But it was a cakewalk for me as I knew how to do it. So, I was able to recall them in both forward and reverse sequence without much difficulty. That's how I came to be called the Memory King by people. Using this method, I have memorised pi's value. Can you guess up to how many digits? No, not a thousand. Not even ten thousand. I recalled pi's value up to thirty-three thousand decimal places just because of these methods and tricks. Now, I am sharing all my secrets with you. With these, you can choose to memorise whatever you wish to.

Overcome Numbers

Phobia

with this Miraculous Method

The Phonetic system associates the digits with various consonant sounds. These consonant sounds can be further combined with vowels to form meaningful words. In this, each digit is represented by one sound or group of sounds. To use the phonetic method, you need to remember this table.

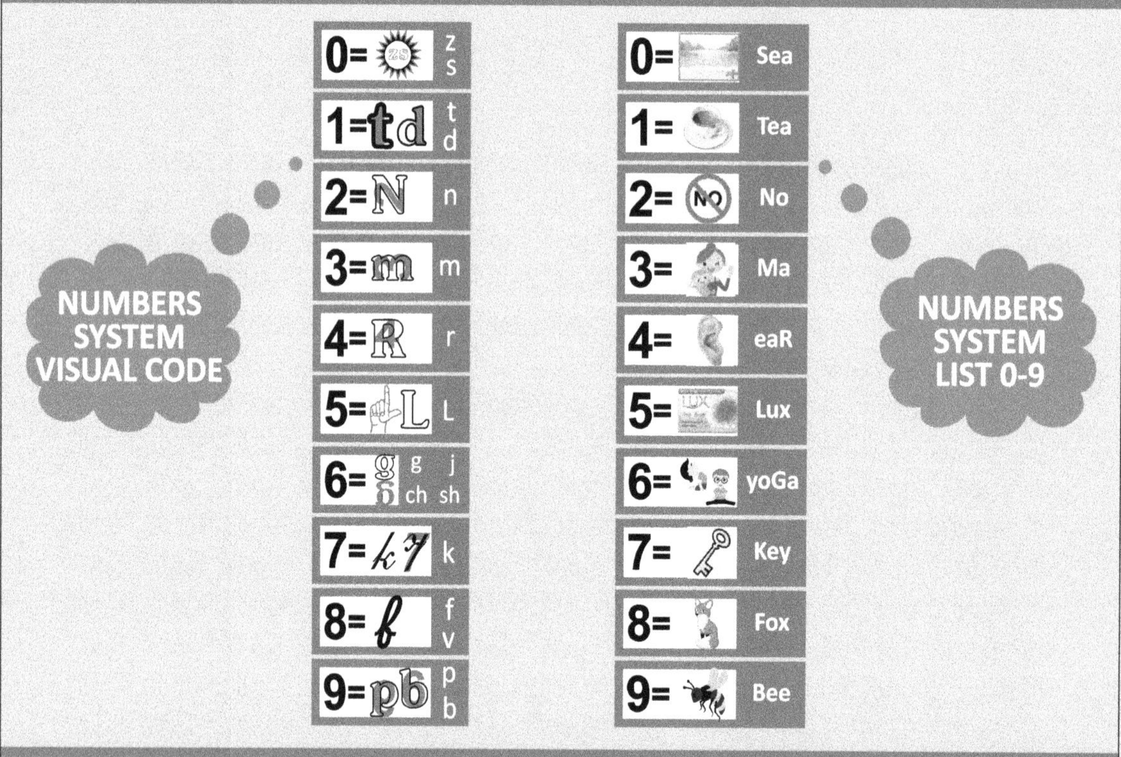

You can see in the image that each digit is assigned one or more alphabets, which are considered its phonetic sound. The consonant sound or code for 0 is z or s, 1—t or d, 2—n, 3—m, 4—r, 5—l, 6—g, j, ch or sh, 7—k, 8—f or v, 9—p or b. I will further simplify these by providing you with tricks to remember them.

To remember that 0 is associated with z or s, you can refer to the word, zero. Its first letter is z. So, that's how you can remember the pair, z and 0. For the pair, s and 0, you can refer to the word, sun. Its shape is that of zero, and its first letter is s. To remember that 1 is associated with t or d, you can refer to their shapes. Shapes of t and d have embedded number 1 in them. In N's shape, you can find the shape of 2 embedded. That's how you can remember the code for 2. In the shape of M, you can see rotated figure 3 easily. In R's shape, you can see the shape of 4. Keep referring to the above image for more clarity. Five fingers make the shape of L when aligned in a form shown in the picture. That's how you can remember the code for 5, i.e., l. I am sharing these tricks so that you can easily memorise these codes. Take a pause here and recall what you have studied till now.

Digit 6 has four codes. You can see that 6's shape is hidden in the letter G and the mirror image of J. For ch, you know six is called chhah in Hindi. So, that's how you can remember ch code for 6. And, you can remember sh with the word six. To memorise the code for 7, i.e., k, remember that K's shape is formed when you combine two 7s with their common point. A lower-case cursive f looks like 8 and in 8's shape, you can find v. So, that's how you can remember the sound or code, f and v for 8. Lastly, 9's code, p and b can be remembered by making certain associations. The mirror image of P resembles 9 and rotating b by 180-degree clockwise forms 9. It's done. Revise and read again and again until it gets printed in your mind. Take a pen and paper and write the sounds or codes ten times. No need to hurry. This is going to benefit you for a lifetime. So, it is worth investing some time in getting hold of them.

Know More

about the
Phonetic Method

What you have studied till now in this chapter will act as your foundation for the future. This will help you to apply the method in various places. To understand it further, see this short and simple example. Suppose you have to remember 99. You can do it by using the phonetic method. The code for 9 is p or b. Choose one, whichever you wish. So, 99's code will be PP or BB. These are written in the upper-case because these codes are considered the main system. The letters you will add in between them to make a meaningful word will be called the supporting system. They will be written in lower-case. So, the word for 99 can be PaPa or BaBa. Note that here a is a supporting letter and P or B is the main letter. Similarly, you can do for 97. Codes for 9 and 7 are B and K, respectively. So, the word can be BiKe. Likewise, you can make meaningful words out of all two digits numbers.

As you have understood the main and supporting system. I will touch upon the right-hand side of the previous image. There, I have derived relevant words from the code of single digits. The main code is in upper-case and the supporting code or letter is in lower-case. Meaningful words for 0 can be Sea, 1—Tea, 2—No, 3—Ma, 4—eaR, 5—Lux, 6—yoGa, 7—Key, 8—Fox, and 9—Bee.

In the next chapter, most of the things will get clear to you. Don't move onto the next chapter until you are very clear with this phonetic method. Otherwise, it won't be easy to understand the upcoming things. Keep revising the codes.

Notes:

The phonetic method is very powerful and helpful:

- Association is made between digits and particular sounds or codes.
- Certain tricks are used to remember the sounds or codes.
- A meaningful word is created for a two-digit number.

CHAPTER 18

'Challenges are what make life interesting and overcoming them is what makes life meaningful.'

—*Joshua J. Marine*

In this chapter, I have provided all the things you need to know to apply the phonetic method. To reduce your burden, I have shared the number system visual code maps. In this, you will get to know the meaningful words that can be created for two-digits numbers starting from 01 till 99 using the phonetic method. These will help you a lot to memorise numbers effortlessly. You will also get to know its varied applications afterwards. But first, sharpen your saw and understand these concepts thoroughly.

CrEATE MEANINGFUL WORDS FOR NUMBER 01 TILL 48

NUMBER SYSTEM VISUAL CODE MAP

Let me tell you how you have to read these images given above. You know about the main and supporting system. The consonant sounds of the digits that you learnt in the last chapter, like 1—t or d, 2—n, etc., are part of the main system. They are written in upper-case. The extra alphabets added to the main system to make a meaningful word out of them are part of the supporting system. They are always written in lower-case.

If you have to create a word for number 01, you will write the sounds or codes for 0 and 1. Sound or code for 0 is s and 1 is t. Therefore, the code for 01 is ST. To make a meaningful word out of ST, you will add some extra letters (supporting system). So, by adding c, o, o, y in ST, ScooTy is formed. The word for 01 is ScooTy. In this way, a picture of scooty will be created in your brain when you read 01.

Similarly, the code for 02 will be SM. By adding small i in-between, SiM is formed, which can be used to remember 02. Likewise, check the images given below till the 48th number. Take a pause and practise these 48 numbers several times. Write them down on paper ten times. Practise reciting them in front of the mirror. Practise them until you are satisfied.

NUMBER SYSTEM VISUAL CODE MAP

Once you have mastered these 48 numbers and made clear pictures of them in your brain, then start working on other numbers. Given below are codes for 49 to 99 numbers. Read and understand them. Practise them again and again. Practise with a partner, in front of a mirror, on a paper. Take self-tests. Pick random numbers and tell the pictures or words associated with them. You will study their applications soon. Before that, these numbers and their pictures should get printed in your mind.

APPLY

THE PHONETIC METHOD TO MEMORISE A SEQUENCE OF NUMBERS

Try To Memorize These Sequence of Complex Number Using Number System Visual Code

51	22	10	54	82
74	88	96	30	52
92	01	37	25	09
61	84	12	04	57
66	52	97	24	56

Now, let us look into one of the applications of this method. You are given 25 two-digits numbers. If you are asked to memorise these—from 51 to 56—how much time will you take? It will be a very boring and complicated process if done by rote learning. But with the phonetic method, you can make it colourful, engaging, easy, and fun. With this method, you can learn as many numbers as you want. That's the beauty of this method.

Three steps need to be followed to memorise these numbers. The first step is to read out all the numbers. The second step is, using the phonetic method, convert numerals into familiar, meaningful words. The last step is to make a story out of all these words. While making a story use the AIR and COMB methods. Also, involve your senses, I-factor, and emotions.

The meaningful words derived using the phonetic method for 51 is oLD, 22—NaNa, 10—Tea-Spoon, 54—LaRa, 82—FM, 74—CaR, 88—FuFa, 96—PiG, 30—MS dhoni, 52—LioN, 92—PeN, 01—ScooTy, 37—MiKe, 25—NaiL, 09—SoaP, 61—GoaT, 84—FiRe, 12—DoN, 04—SiR, 57—LaKe, 66—eGG, 52—LioN, 97—BiKe, 24—NRi, and 56—LeG. You can write these words below the numbers on the book or a separate paper for your ease.

Now, make a story using all these words. Your story can be somewhat like this, my oLD NaNa was given medicine in Tea Spoon by LaRa dutta. She went to put the FM on in the CaR in which my FuFa (uncle) was sitting with a PiG and MS dhoni. He saw a LioN on the road, took his camera embedded PeN out and grabbed a ScooTy to announce with a MiKe about the lion. Using his NaiLs and SoaP, lion was eating a GoaT. Someone threw FiRe ball on it. DoN and SiR shooed it away. The lion went to a LaKe and ate an eGG with another LioN. Then, on a BiKe, NRi came and lion Bit him on his LeG. Now, re-read the story and keep the numbers and their codes in mind. From the story, you can easily derive the numbers. This is how you can memorise numbers smartly.

TAKE A
SELF-ASSESSMENT
TEST

Once you have understood the above story, try to put the numbers in the forward and reverse sequence in the below-provided space.

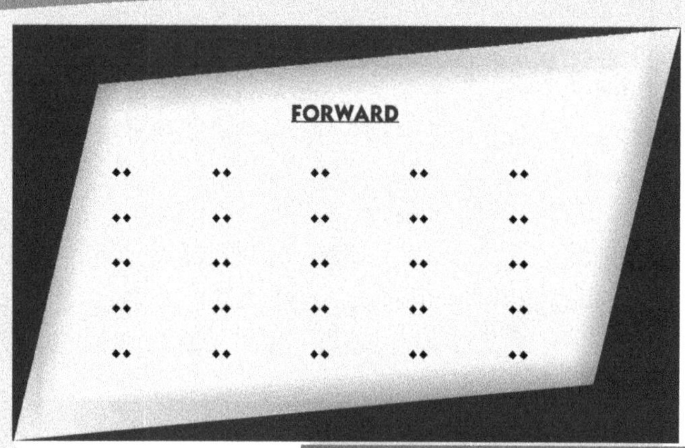

Notes:

Using the three-step formula, the phonetic method can be applied efficiently:

- Read out all the numbers.
- Make meaningful words out of the numbers using the sounds or codes.
- Create an exciting story using all the words to memorise all the numbers.

CHAPTER 19

STORE ALL ESSENTIAL NUMBERS AND DATES IN PERMANENT MEMORY

'The idea is to use it or lose it, work out your brain cells so that they can stay active and healthy.'

—Gary Small

We have an amazing, limitless brain but unfortunately, we are not exploring and utilising it enough. Just like the body needs some exercise to stay in shape and remain fit and active, the brain also requires specific exercises to stay active throughout life. Unfortunately, people, rather than relying on their brains, depend on gadgets to remember things. This way, they underestimate the powers of the brain.

By applying these memorisation methods in real life, you will be able to remember most things even in old age. It is a struggle to remember phone numbers, house numbers, Aadhar card number, account numbers, dates of events, etc. But now you will enjoy learning these things. This will increase your confidence and social image. You will start to love this process of memorising numbers and details. People will get easily impressed by you—when you will effortlessly recall their phone numbers, birth dates, house numbers, ID card numbers, etc. Everything is possible in this memory world—you need to be willing to learn and explore.

Remember Forever

TRY TO MEMORIZE THESE HOUSE AND PHONE NUMBERS USING NUMBER SYSTEM VISUAL CODE

HOUSE NUMBERS

Sonia	C - 314
Diksha	G - 97
Amit	B - 147

PHONE NUMBERS

Gaurav	011-33478451
My Cell No.	9313974850, 9718269182

As you can see in the above picture, house numbers and phone numbers are given. You are supposed to memorise them. The first part contains the names of people, and the second part contains pictureless letters or numbers. Whenever you see an unfamiliar name, what do you do? Yes! You use the PNN method. Remember that initially, every new task seems difficult, but once you understand the concept and start applying it—it will become very easy for you. Therefore, having patience while learning these concepts is very important.

To memorise the house numbers, first, read them out. Mostly the names of the house owner will be familiar to you. So, you won't have to give special nicknames to them. But here, you can give nicknames as they are unfamiliar names. The first data is of Sonia. Sonia's nickname can be, Sonia Gandhi. For the house number part, the letter can be memorised using the PNN method and numbers can be memorised using the phonetic method. So, C's nickname can be, cat. To use the phonetic method on 314, you need to divide the number into pairs, as it is used on single or double digits. Hence, you can divide 314 into 31 and 4. You know that the code for 31 is MaT. To memorise the single digit, you can use either the shape, rhyme, or phonetic methods. The easiest one to use is the rhyme method. For 4, the rhyming word will be, door. Sonia, C, 31, and 4 become Sonia Gandhi, cat, MaT, and door, respectively. By using the link method, you can create a short story like, Sonia Gandhi is keeping an eye on my cat who is sitting on her MaT near the door. With this single sentence, you can easily remember the owner and house number. I can assure you that these techniques will be immensely useful to you, once you get a hold of them. Just don't stop in-between. Keep trying and applying them.

Coming to the phone numbers, Gaurav's number is 01133478451. To memorise this number using the phonetic method, you need to divide it into pairs, convert each pair into words, and then make a short story. The meaningful word for 01 can be, SuiT, 13—DaM, 34—MoR (peacock), 78—CoFfee, 45—RaiL, and 1—gun (using the rhyme method). Their one-liner story can be like, SuiT was kept ready on the DaM for MoR, while he was drinking CoFfee on the RaiL with his gun. The next number is mine (not actually mine). It's 9313974850. Each pair can be converted to a meaningful word using the phonetic method. Word or code for 93 can be, PM, 13—DaM, 97—BiKe, 48—RooF, and 50—LaSsi. Their one-liner story can be somewhat like this, to meet PM, I went to the secret DaM with my super BiKe after crossing the RooF and packing LaSsi for him. I have learnt thousands of phone numbers using this method. You can do it too. You can easily remember phone numbers and utilise both sides of your brain by putting these theories into practice. Involve your senses, I-factor, and emotions while ridiculously associating and imagining these names and stories.

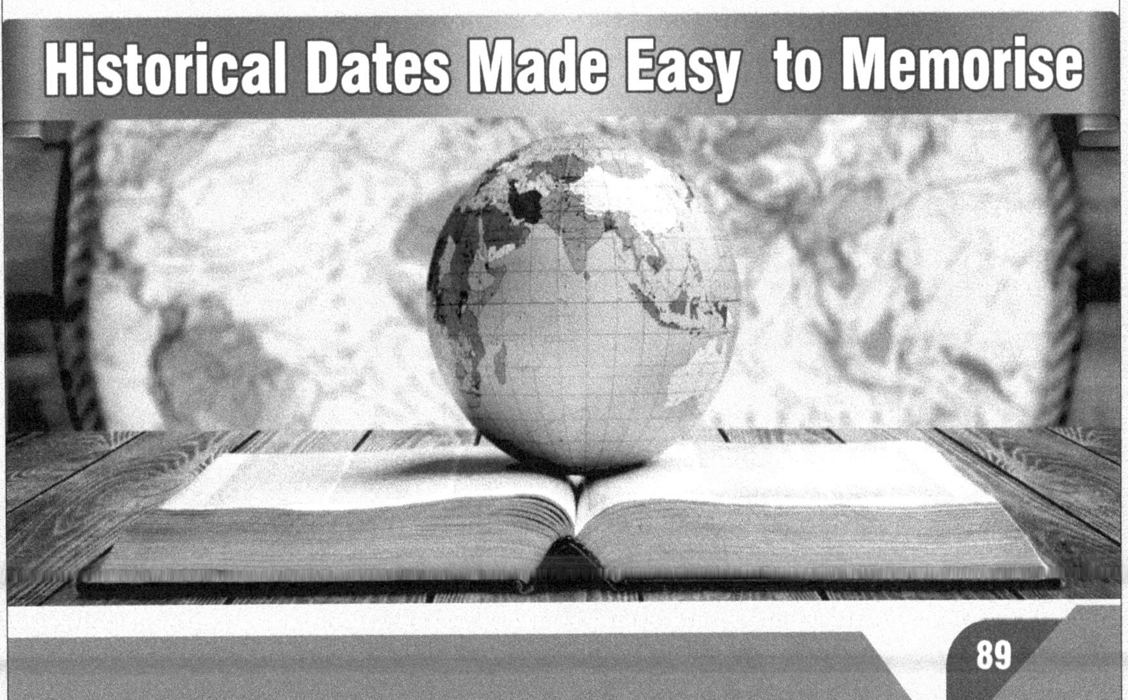

TRY TO MEMORIZE THESE HISTORICAL DATES USING NUMBER SYSTEM VISUAL CODE

Date	Event
1707	Death of Aurangzeb
1757	Battle of Plassey
1772	Birth of Raja Ram Mohan Roy
1780	First newspaper was published
1817	Hindu college was established in Kolkata
1824	Birth of Swami Dayanand
1825	Birth of Dadabhai Naoroji
1828	Establishment of Brahmo Samaj
1869	Birth of Mahatma Gandhi.
1919	Jallianwala Bagh Massacre.

With these methods, you can easily remember the dates of historical events in an interesting and longer-lasting manner. Firstly, read out all the details given in the picture. Most students tend to remember or guess the first half of the date but not the second half. For example, in 1707, the first half, 17 is mostly familiar but not the second half, 07. So, you can use the phonetic method to learn the second half. You can use the phonetic method to learn the first half as well.

In 1707, Aurangzeb died. To remember this event, you can use the combination of phonetic, PNN, and link methods. The second half of 1707, 07 can be converted into SKy, using the phonetic method. Death of Aurangzeb's nickname can be, death orange jeb (pocket). Using the link method, they can be linked by saying, SKy se girne se death hogyi orange ki, isliye usne usse jeb mai rakh lia (orange died after falling from the sky, so he kept it in his pocket). In 1757, the battle of Plassey took place. 57 can be converted into LaKe. Battle of Plassey's nickname can be, bottle plastic. Their one-liner story can be, LaKe is full of invisible bottles made up of plastic. In 1772, Raja Ram Mohan Roy was born. 72 can be converted into KNeel. The event's nickname can be, birthday of Raja, Ram, and Mohan. Their one-liner story can be, he KNeeled on the birthday of Raja, Ram, and Mohan to wish them. In 1780, the first newspaper was published. 80 can be converted into FiSh. The event and date can be linked by saying, FiSh is reading its first newspaper. In 1817, Hindu college was established in Kolkata. 17 can be converted into DucK. The event's nickname can be, college coal. Their short story can be, DucK established its college on coal.

In 1824, Swami Dayanand was born. 24 can be converted into NaRi (woman). Event's nickname can be, birthday of Daya and Anand. Their short story can be like, NaRi (woman) celebrated the birthday of her children, Daya and Anand. In 1825, Dadabhai Naoroji was born. 25 can be converted into NaiL. The event's nickname can be, birthday of dada, bhai, and nanaji. Their one-liner story can be, he cut the NaiL of everyone, on the birthday of dada, bhai, and nanaji. In 1828, Brahmo Samaj was established. 28 can be converted into NaaV (boat). The event's nickname can be, Brahma aaj (today). Their one-liner story can be, Bhagwan Brahma aaj NaaV par puri dunia ghumenge (Lord Brahma will roam the world on a boat today). In 1969, Mahatma Gandhi was born. 69 can be converted into JeeP. The event's nickname can be, Gandhi's baby. Their short story can be, Gandhi's baby drove the JeeP by himself. In 1919, the Jallianwala Bagh massacre took place. 19 can be converted into DeePak (lamp). Event and date can be linked by saying, DeePak was lit to mourn the Jallianwala Bagh massacre. Take a short break and recall what the events and dates were. What happened in 1772? When was Mahatma Gandhi born? Ask such questions to yourself to master them.

Try To Memorize These Historical Dates Using Number System Visual Code

Date	Event
1927	TV Demonstration for the first time.
1964	Nehru passes away Shastri becomes the Prime minister.
1921	Mahatma Gandhi Joined Congress leadership.
1922	Chauri-Chaura incidence.
1930	First Round Table conference.
1952	First General Elections held.
1972	Shimla Agreement signed.
1498	Vasco da Gama lands at Calicut.

It's time to practise. First, memorise the above dates and events. After this, take it as a challenge to memorise your account number, friends and family members' phone numbers, and other significant numbers. Then, impress people by showcasing your newly developed superpower.

Notes:

Important numbers, dates, and events can be remembered using memorisation techniques:

- Use the phonetic method to convert numbers or dates into meaningful words.
- Utilise the rhyme method to memorise a single digit.
- Apply the PNN method to remember names.

CHAPTER 20

Learn Lengthy Texts Instantly

'We've forgotten how to remember, and just as importantly, we've forgotten how to pay attention. So, instead of using your smartphone to jot down crucial notes, or googling an elusive fact, use every opportunity to practice your memory skills. Memory is a muscle, to be exercised and improved.'

—Joshua Foer

Memorising long chapters and answers is seen as a very hectic task. It is, no doubt, difficult to memorise when done by rote learning and traditional way. But it can be made very simple to memorise just by using some memorisation techniques. In this chapter, I will tell you, step by step, how to remember lengthy information in a way that you can recall that easily during exams.

It will be a three-step process to memorise lengthy information. In the first step, you will be required to read and understand the text and mark the keywords attentively. Keywords are those that tell you about the main idea of something. The keyword is the most critical word in a sentence, and it is the crux of the given data. Therefore, it is crucial to understand the text before moving on to the next step. Understanding it correctly will complete half of your task. The second step will be to write down those keywords in the correct sequence on a paper. The third step is to memorise those keywords using any of the methods that you have learnt till now.

Students waste a lot of time and effort by trying to memorise every word and unimportant data. This should not be done. Instead, they should focus on only keywords and not the complete sentence. By learning the keywords, they can easily make sentences using them in the exam.

I have written fifteen keywords from a long question based on the properties of plastic in the below image. First, I read and understood the question and its answer carefully, then marked the keywords and finally noted them down. Noting the keywords of the question is also essential. To memorise this, you can use the story, shape, rhyme, or phonetic method. Here, I will use the rhyme method to learn them quickly and recall them instantly in the exam. You may use any method you are comfortable with. Most of the words or phrases have some pictures associated with them in your brain. If they were pictureless, then you could have used the PNN method to associate images with them.

Plastic and its properties

1. Light in Weight
2. Good Insulator
3. Corrosion Resistive
4. Easy Workability
5. Adhesiveness
6. Low Fabrication Cost
7. Good Strength
8. Easy Molding
09. Insect Resistant
10. Converted into desired shape
11. Chemical Inertness
12. Transparency
13. Low Melting Point
14. Low Maintenance Cost
15. Dimensional Stability

The first keyword is light in weight. One rhymes with gun. They can be linked by saying, I have a huge plastic gun which is very light in weight. The second is good insulator. Two rhymes with shoe, and the nickname for good insulator can be, good shoe leta (lie). Their short story can be, voh good boy ek bade shoe mai leta hua hai (that good boy is lying down in a big shoe). The third is corrosion resistive. Three rhymes with tree. Their short story can be, my plastic tree never corrodes; it resists all changes. The fourth is easy workability. Four rhymes with door, chor (thief), or mor (choose any rhyming word you like). Their short story can be, that chor does his work quickly at night and steals away all money. The fifth is adhesiveness. Five rhymes with hive. You can say, he uses honey from hive as adhesive. The sixth is low fabrication cost. Six rhymes with bricks or sticks. To remember them, you can say, bricks have a low cost of making. The seventh is good strength. Seven rhymes with heaven. Their short story can be like, people in heaven have good physical and mental strength. The eighth is easy moulding. Eight rhymes with skates. To remember them, you can say, my skates are easily moldable in any shape. Recall what you have studied till here before moving forward.

Coming to the next column, the ninth keyword is insect resistant. Nine rhymes with wine. Their short story can be, insects are resistant to wine's effects. The tenth is converted into the desired shape. Ten rhymes with hen. They can be remembered by saying, a hen wrote that it wants to be converted into a dog's shape so that people don't consider her food. The eleventh is chemical inertness. Eleven rhymes with lemon. Their short story can be, lemon makes all chemicals inert or inactive. The twelfth is transparency. Twelve rhymes with shelves. Their short story can be, all of his shelves are transparent and very costly. The thirteenth is a low melting point. Thirteen rhymes with hurting. Their short story can be, everyone was hurting him and making him feel low by pointing fingers at him. The fourteenth is low maintenance cost. Fourteen rhymes with Mortein. They can be remembered by saying, Mortein is low in cost and requires less maintenance. The fifteenth is dimensional stability. Fifteen rhymes with fitting. Their short story can be, diamond fitted in plastic nicely and improved its stability. Recall the keywords without looking at them.

To remember such keywords, you can use the shape method by associating the shapes of numbers with the corresponding keywords or you can use the phonetic method by converting the digits into meaningful words and linking them with keywords. Also, you can use the story method easily in such cases. However, you may prefer the rhyme and shape methods when the keywords are less in number. And use the phonetic and story method when the keywords are more in number.

Notes:
Long chapters can be very smartly memorised using different techniques:
- Read and understand the text and mark the keywords.
- Write down the keywords in forward sequence on paper.
- Use the shape, rhyme, phonetic, or story method to memorise them.

CHAPTER 21

Memorise Anything using the Memorisation Techniques

'Success is the sum of small efforts, repeated day in and day out.'

—Robert Collier

In this chapter, you will learn to apply the previously learnt methods to different areas—such as memorising elements and their atomic numbers, melting point; spellings of difficult words; word meanings; names of phobias, etc.

I can very well empathise with students and their studies-related problems, as I was a below-average student and faced a lot of difficulties in my studies. But these methods taken from the Vedas made me Memory King and improved my performance unbelievably. After exploring and learning all techniques for thirteen years, I have compiled this book for you. I want to contribute something to your life, and I hope these techniques will be useful for you.

Rule over the World of Elements

Sodium	11	Tin	50
Potassium	19	Antimony	51
Chromium	24	Europium	63
Iron	26	Tungsten	74
Nickel	28	Gold	79
Arsenic	33	Lead	82
Krypton	36	Radium	88
Cadmium	48		

Though I am sure you have already memorised the periodic table, but I want you to master all its related information using the PNN, phonetic, and link methods. So, firstly, read out all the data. Then associate pictures with pictureless words using the phonetic method and convert numbers to meaningful words. Then finally, link them using the link method.

Consider the left-hand side list first. The nickname for sodium can be, soda. 11 can be converted to DaDa (grandfather). So, their link can be, my DaDa drinks soda ten times a day. To simplify this process for you, I have mentioned the nickname of each word that you can make and the meaningful word that can you can create from each number in brackets next to them. The short story for potassium (pot) and 19 (DeePak) can be, I daily lit DeePak in a pot; chromium (crow) and 24 (NaRi [women])—NaRi was picked up by a big crow; iron (iron press) and 26 (NaG [snake])—he flattened the NaG with iron press; nickel (Nick) and 28 (NaaV [boat])—Nick crossed all the oceans in the world with his small NaaV; Arsenic (sainik [soldier]) and 33 (MaMa [uncle])—All my MaMa are sainik; krypton (captain) and 36 (MuG)—the captain has his photo imprinted on every crew's mugs; cadmium (Cadbury) and 48 (RooF)—I kept all my Cadbury chocolates on the roof to hide from siblings. Now, take a pause and recall all the elements and their atomic numbers.

Now, work on the right-hand side list. Read all the given information. The short stories for tin and 50 (LaSsi) can be, I drank ten tin cans filled with LaSsi nonstop; antimony (aunty money) and 51 (LoTa [container])—my aunty kept all her money in LoTa which got stolen; europium (rope) and 63 (JaM)—while skipping rope, I always eat JaM bread; tungsten (tongue) and 74 (KaR [car])—he cleaned the dust on KaR with his tongue; gold and 79 (KaP [cap])—I wear gold studded KaPs only; lead (lead pencil) and 82 (FaN)—he wrote his name with his lead pencil on all my FaNs; radium (radio) and 88 (FiFa)—everyone gathered to hear FiFa updates on an old radio.

The speciality of the phonetic method is that it can be used for more than two digits numbers. You can easily use it to remember the melting points of various elements. Suppose you have to memorise the melting point of an element which is 1950 degrees Celsius, then you can convert 1950 into a meaningful word. The code for 1950 will be TBLS. The meaningful word from that can be derived from this can be, TaBLeS. So, you can link that element with TaBLeS by saying, all my TaBLeS are made up of that element.

Similarly, the code for the melting point of lead, 327 degrees Celsius, will be MNK. Its meaningful word can be, MoNKey. Their short story can be, with his lead pencil, he made Mahatma Gandhi's three MoNKeys. In this way, you can memorise the atomic numbers, masses, melting points, boiling points, and many more values of the elements or compounds.

SMART MEMORY FOR SPELLING

Try to find the letter which is more confusing and then see that very big (5-6 times) of the confusing letter. What's the Spelling of 12th?

Many of you Answer that Twelth, Tweleth, both are wrong and the correct one is Twelfth.

Here, F is confusing.
So, try to make F big and big.

Twel **f** th

Students generally face issues in writing correct spellings. I have a way for you, with which you can memorise the commonly misspelt words. Whenever you are confused by the presence of a particular letter in the word then write that letter in bold or uppercase. You can also encircle it. Then write that word five times. Suppose you want to remember that the spelling of 12th contains f in it. Then write f in uppercase in the spelling of 12th—twelFth. And write it five times on paper.

SMART MEMORY FOR SPELLING

Pseudonym

g**H**ost

Psychology

r**H**etorical

A similar trick can be used for silent letters present in a word. Focus on the letter which is commonly misspelt or ignored. If you are confused with principle and principal, then write princi**PLE** and princi**PAL** in this way, five times.

SMART MEMORY FOR SPELLING

Princi**pal** and Princi**ple**

To remember the spelling of judgement, mark a tick on judgement and mark a big cross sign on jugment (mistakenly considered as right spelling) as shown in the above picture. Do the same for develop and develope.

Memorise Word Meanings

Like Never Before

TRY TO MEMORIZE THESE WORDS AND MEANINGS USING PNN METHOD.

Word	Meaning
Capacious	Huge, Roomy
Cajole	To flatter
Encroach	To enter without permission
Elective	Selective
Immutable	Stable
Surly	Rudely, In a rude manner
Skinflint	A miser Person
Extirpate	Remove something unwanted

Many of my students are working on learning the entire dictionary. I love to guide such enthusiastic students. You can also memorise entire books or dictionaries using these methods. You also have that potential. Words and their meanings are a common topic in exams. They can be memorised without any difficulty using various techniques.

Suppose you have to learn the meaning of capacious which is, huge. You can give a nickname to capacious as, cap. Then, connect it with its meaning by saying, he wore such a huge cap that its weight did not allow him to move. Next is cajole. Cajole means to flatter. Their nicknames can be, Kajol and flat respectively.

They can be linked by saying, Kajol is living in her flat in Delhi. Encroach means to enter without permission. Its nickname can be, cockroach. It can be linked to its meaning by saying, cockroach entered my room without permission.

Elective means selective. Elective's nickname can be, active and selective's nickname can be, select. Their short story can be, super active people are only selected for this job. Immutable means stable. Immutable's nickname can be, table. It can be linked to its meaning by saying, this table is extremely stable, even an elephant can't move it. Surly means rudely. Surly's nickname can be, sir. It can be linked to its meaning in this way, sir always talks to him rudely. Skinflint means a miser (kanjus) person. Skinflint's nickname can be, skin and miser's nickname can be, kanjus. They can be linked by saying, voh kanjus insaan khane mai itna kum khata hai ki uski skin se uski bones dikhane lagi hai (that misery person eats so little that his bones have started showing from his skin). Extirpate means remove something unwanted. Extirpate's nickname can be, extra pet (stomach). It can be linked to its meaning by a short sentence, he wants to remove the unwanted extra pet. Now, cover the meanings portion in the image with your hand and recall the meanings by looking at the word. You will be glad that using these simple methods, you are able to memorise these words in one go.

Names of phobias are pretty confusing and complicated. It is often difficult for students to remember them but not for the students who have studied the memorisation techniques. By associating and visualising the phobias in a ridiculous way, they can be remembered for a lifetime. Acrophobia is the fear of heights. Acrophobia's nickname can be, a crow. It can be linked to its meaning with this short story, a crow grabbed my shirt and flown me to a high altitude that instilled fear in me. Limnophobia means fear of lakes. Limnophobia's nickname can be, lemon. It can be related to its meaning with this short story, huge lemon is fearful of drowning

NEVER STOP PRACTISING

TRY TO MEMORIZE THESE WORDS AND MEANINGS USING PNN METHOD.

Word	Meaning
Assinine	Stupid
Ameliorate	To improve
Burgeon	To expand
Candid	Honest
Certitude	To be sure
Despondency	Hopeless
Fester	To irritate
Flux	To change
Dilligent	Hardworking
Frail	Easily breakable state

Now, practise and apply what you have learnt till now. Only practise and revision can make your concepts stronger and turn you into a memory master. So practise as much as possible, as this one-time investment of effort can give you lifetime benefits.

Notes:

Memorisation techniques are highly useful:

- Elements and their specifications can be learnt easily.
- Spellings and word meanings can be memorised without difficulty.
- Complex and confusing names of phobias can be made easy to remember.

CHAPTER 22

STUDY TECHNIQUES

'Research shows that you begin learning in the womb and go right on learning until the moment you pass on. Your brain has a capacity for learning that is virtually limitless, which makes every human a potential genius.'

—Michael J. Gelb

In this chapter, I will scientifically and systematically discuss the six top things that you should set before starting your studies or work to get the best result in the shortest time. They will make you highly productive and effective. To get the most out of them, write the essential points on paper and stick the paper near your study place. This will act as a constant reminder for you.

Teachers and parents tell students to study by concentrating the mind, but they don't tell them how to do that. Bhagavad Gita says that the mind can be our best friend or worst enemy, depending on who controls whom. If you let your mind control and dictate you, then you become its puppet and deteriorate with time. But if you control it and make it do what you want to, then you can achieve unbelievable success. Therefore, it is crucial to control the mind. Otherwise, it will keep jumping from one thing to another like a monkey.

There are two major ways to set the mind correctly. First is, answer to what and why. Maximum people don't know what they want from life, what they want to become, and why they want—what they desire. They are easily influenced by friends, parents, and society and start copying what they are doing without understanding their uniqueness. This is a big hurdle in the path to success.

A train before leaving knows its destination, that's why it reaches there on time. If a person does not know his destination, purpose of life, right direction, then where will he reach? He will get distracted very easily and will end up wasting a lot of time. Your what and why will motivate you to work and study. After knowing them, you won't need external motivation. They will wake you up on time, make you study for longer hours, and keep you focused. UPSC or any other exams toppers are crystal clear about what and why they want; that's what make them successful. The more benefits or answers to whys you are able to extract from what, the more you will be drawn to achieve your goal.

I want you to be crystal clear about your answers to what and why. Take a break from the world for half an hour, go to a quiet place, take a pen, and write down your strengths, uniqueness, interests, and goals. Think deeply and write down what you want out of life and why you want it. It is a gradual process to figure out these things; it won't happen in one go. So, don't worry, take your time, and sit daily to think about it. Ask for help from God and dear ones. You will get the proper guidance. Before starting studying, take out five minutes or so to visualise your goals and purpose. Do this visualisation practice after waking up, before sleeping, and when you feel distracted. This will align you on the right path.

The second and the most important way to set the mind is by mediating. Meditation is amazing and its benefits are endless. From time immemorial, meditation is being practised. By concentrating the mind on God and chanting his names, you can purify and set your mind. The sages and saints were able to become calmer, happier, and more focused by meditating. Therefore, you should always set aside some time to meditate to set your mind and soul right.

SET YOUR BRAIN

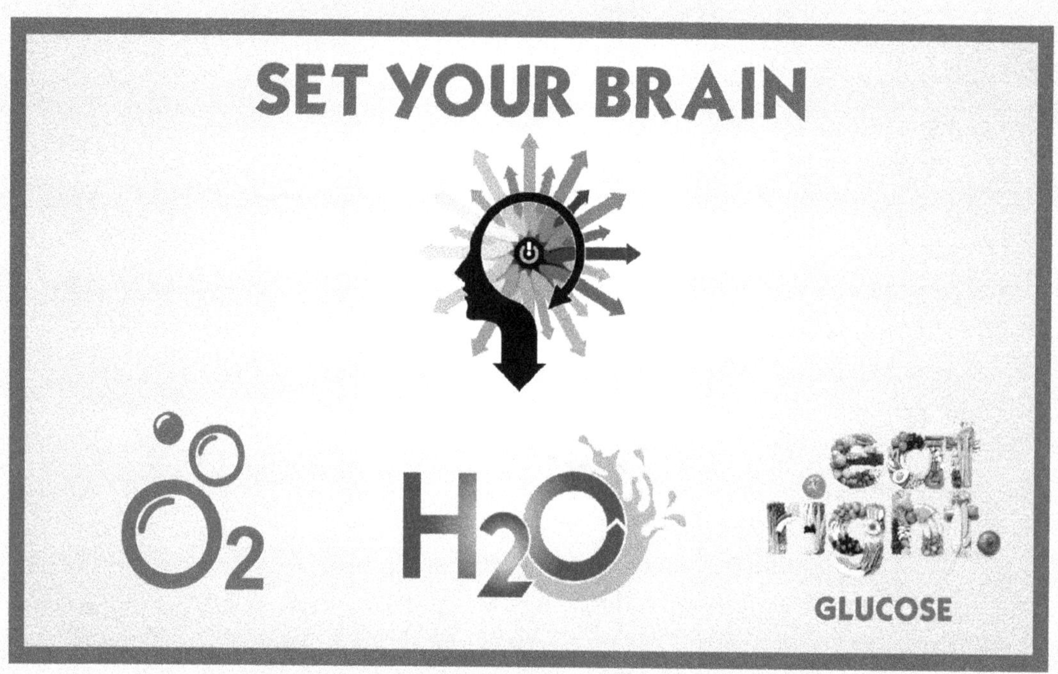

If you consider your mind to be software, then your brain is hardware. The brain has its own needs and requirements. It is necessary to fulfil them to get the best performance. It requires three things—oxygen, water, and glucose. Oxygen is vital for the brain to work correctly. The optimum oxygen level can be maintained by doing the pranayama (breathing exercises) and taking morning walks in the fresh air. Water is another necessity of the brain. There is 75% water in your brain. This shows the importance of water for the brain. While studying or working, you should always keep a water bottle by your side and keep drinking it throughout the day. Water refreshes the brain and improves its effectiveness. Any other drink cannot replace it. Therefore, you should drink 2-3 litres of water every day. Another essential thing for your brain is glucose, i.e., food. You should eat homemade sattvic food to nourish your brain. Sattvic food includes clean, fresh, healthy, plant-based food. It includes fruits, vegetables, nuts, legumes, milk and milk products, etc. Limit junk food and soft drinks to increase the brain's powers.

Your body has a direct link to your studies. You must have noticed when you are ill; you are not able to study. Your body's posture, health, and strength impact your studies and work significantly. You should always prioritise your health over other things. Follow the 20/20/20 rule to become successful in all dimensions. Give 20 minutes to meditation to set your mind, 20 minutes to pranayama to set your brain, and 20 minutes to exercise to set your body. By investing one hour for yourself, you will prepare your mind, brain, and body for the rest twenty-three hours of the day. Remember that all these three steps are equally important, don't skip any of them. Initially, you can start with 5-5-5, i.e., give 5 minutes to each activity. Then, shift to 10 minutes, then 20 minutes.

You should try to involve most of your senses—visual (seeing), auditory (hearing), tactile (touch), gustatory (taste), and olfactory (smell)—while studying or working on getting the most out of your studies and work. Speak, watch, hear, and feel what you are studying. Stay in the present. Purify your sense by nourishing them with good inputs to get good outputs. By listening, speaking, and watching spiritual and moral content, your senses get set and cleansed. This makes you a better student, professional, and, most importantly, a good human.

Set your Place

Most people don't know the importance of setting their study or work place. You should have a fixed place for studies or work. Let's understand this by some examples. When you go to the gym, you see the equipment and other people working out, then you also feel like exercising. When you see a temple, smell the aroma of incense sticks, feel the aura, hear the sound of bells, then your hands automatically come together to pray; you feel peaceful and contented. When you pass by a restaurant, your mouth waters, and you feel hungry. When you visit a library and see others studying, you also become serious towards studies and feel like studying. This is how your body's system work. The aura or the surroundings of a particular place makes you think or do what it is meant for. This fact can be used for your study place as well. You should have a separate study space. If you study at the place of eating or sleeping, you will feel hungry or sleepy. So, you should strictly keep the place for studying to study only. No other activity such as using a phone, watching TV or Netflix, eating, taking naps, etc., should be done there.

When the timing of a particular activity is fixed, your body and mind stay prepared to perform it. That's how they do the task in coordination with each other and in a smooth manner. For example, if your dinner time is fixed at 8 p.m., you will automatically feel hungry at 8 p.m. If your sleeping time is 11 p.m., then you will feel sleepy at that time every day. Similarly, you should keep a fixed study time so that you feel like studying every day at the same time. You should prefer the morning time or Brahma Muhurta to study, as you are the most energetic and fresh during that time. It's the best time to study. There is no disturbance or noise, and your willpower is maximum. To include this in your habits, do this continuously for twenty-one days without a break. If, by chance, you break the rhythm, then start again from day one.

To maximise your result, you should set your mind, brain, body, senses, place, and time. Firstly, know what and why you want to do a particular activity. Then, take the help of meditation—to fulfil your purpose, increase focus, connect with the divine, seek God's help, and stay happy and satisfied always. Control your mind, but don't let your mind control you. Take oxygen, water, and glucose sufficiently for the proper functioning of your brain—exercise to keep your body fit. Use the 20/20/20 formula to keep your mind, brain, and body fit and active. Purify your senses and keep them under control. Set a particular place only for studying, don't do anything else there. Set your daily schedule and fix your study time. By following these tips, you can see a massive positive change in your personality, studies, career, and every other area of life.

CHAPTER 23

Use Powerful Study Secrets to Change your

'That which we persist in doing becomes easier for us to do; not that the nature of the thing itself is changed, but that our power to do is increased.'

—*Ralph Waldo Emerson*

In this chapter, you will get to know the deep study secrets, which, when applied to studies and work, can improve your performance by 500%. They can bring a massive change in you. These tips and tricks will guide you in the journey to achieve unbelievable success. Write the important points on a separate paper and stick it near your study place—to get the maximum results.

Space Learning

Usually, students tend to study continuously without taking a break. This way, they get tired and bored easily. I am often asked by students in my seminars, schools and colleges' workshops, in the YouTube comments section, about the right way of scheduling. They complain that they want to study for longer hours continuously but are not able to do so. If you have similar issues, then space learning will be quite useful to you. Space learning is a great way to schedule your study time. In this, you divide three hours of study time into three parts of one hour each. Then divide that one hour into two parts of fifty and ten minutes each. Fifty minutes are assigned for studying, and the rest ten minutes are given for a break. Students generally neglect the break part, thinking it is a waste of time. But they are unaware of the importance of taking a break.

Your heart doesn't pump blood continuously; it does that in breaks. It pumps, then rests, then pumps again. Similarly, taking a break after studies is very important. It allows the information gained till now to get absorbed. It relaxes the brain and prepares it for the upcoming study session. So, from now on, you can study for fifty minutes, then take a ten-minutes and continue this cycle. You can use a timer to remind you of the break. During breaks, try to avoid using your phone, laptop, or TV as they will strain your eyes and brain. You can walk, exercise, stretch, talk to family members, meditate, do breathing exercises, visualise, etc. This is the secret behind efficient learning for longer hours.

To achieve more than others, you have to put effort more than others. Rather than directly jumping from one topic to another, you can invest an extra one-third of the learning time in gathering more information about what you studied. Suppose you read a topic for fifteen minutes, don't directly move to the next topic. Invest one-third, in this case, five minutes to research more about that topic to gain mastery over it. This will strengthen your concepts, make you more knowledgeable, confident, etc. Remember that extra efforts lead to extra results.

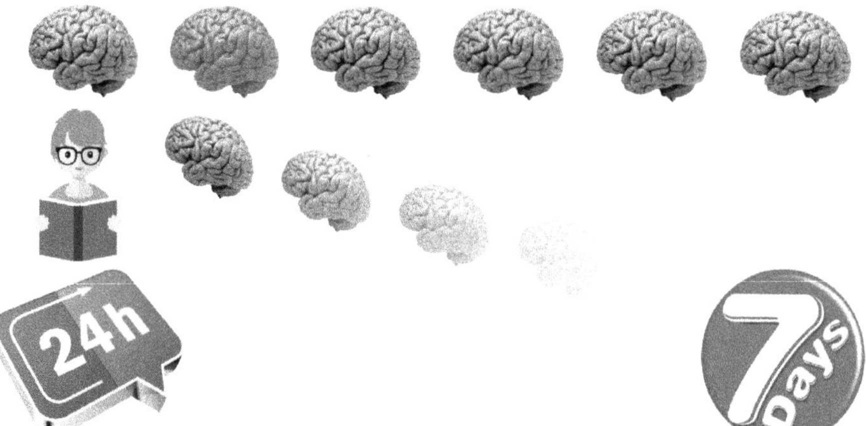

In most of my interactions with students, they complain that they forget what they have studied, especially in the examination hall. The scientifically researched plan that I will share will help you to overcome this problem. According to researches, three types of revisions should be done within a particular time frame. The first revision of what you have studied should be done within twenty-four hours of studies. If you do so, then you will remember that for the next seven days and will be able to recall easily. If you don't do so, then your first forgetting cycle will start, and you will forget the major part of your studies by the seventh day. After that, the second forgetting cycle will start. The second revision should be done within seven days. This allows you to retain the information for the next thirty days. The third revision should be done within a month. This will put the information in your long-term memory, and you will remember that for a lifetime. This is how you can plan your revision. But most students don't revise in this scientifically researched manner, due to which they tend to forget crucial information, especially during exams.

Now, the question is, at what time you should revise? As your brain has the highest energy level in the morning, you can allocate that time for learning new and important concepts. As revision does not take much effort, you can use the time before sleeping as revision time. For the second revision, Sunday can be considered as a revision day where learning new things can be avoided. On Sunday, whatever you have studied from Monday to Saturday can be revised. If you take one hour to study a topic, then to revise it the first time, you will take only about twelve minutes. And second revision will take about ten minutes, and the third will take around seven minutes. The time taken in revision reduces gradually. But if you don't follow this three revisions strategy, then you will end up wasting a lot of time. The reason being, if you read what you have studied without revising it within twenty-four hours, it will take the same time as it took when you studied it for the first time. Then, it can't be called re-vision; it will become re-reading, which is not useful.

Reintegration

REINTEGRATION

After working hard the entire year, after seeing the question papers, students forget the answer even after studying it before. This creates panic in them as they start forgetting other answers and degrade their performance. That's why students should never panic in such situations. Rather, they should handle them in a better way.

When you go from one room to the other to search for something, but you forget what you were searching for, then by tracing the path back, you can recall the forgotten thing. You can use this trick in your examination hall as well. When you forget the answer, stay calm, sit quietly, and visualise. Visualise the past—when you read about that topic, sitting in your room with the book open. Try to trace back the path. In this way, your brain will get a trigger that will help to recall the answer. By visualising the past, you will be able to retrieve the information stored deep inside the brain. This is called reintegration. This is a highly useful method to recall the forgotten information.

INTERFERENCE

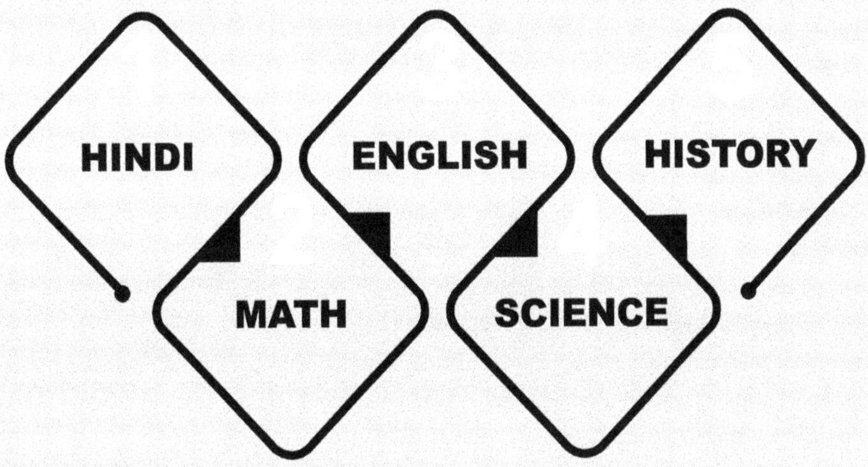

Students generally ask me whether they should study one subject in a day or study multiple subjects. My advice always is to keep changing subjects. When you read one subject continuously for many hours, you involve only one portion of your brain—which develops pressure on that area. This leads to boredom and frustration. Therefore, to keep up the energy and interest levels, you can study one logical and one theoretical subject in a day. Logical subjects are like Maths, Science, etc., where you have to think, apply logic, and then answer. In contrast, theoretical subjects are like English, Hindi, History, etc., where a lot of theory and rote learning are involved—making a combination of these two leads to better performance. This is called interference. By combining space learning and interference, you can make the most out of your studies.

So, you should know the importance of breaks. Always involve breaks in between the study sessions. You can study for fifty minutes then take ten minutes break. Invest one-third of your time in researching more about what you have read. Plan your revision sessions properly. Follow the three revisions method. Revise within twenty-four hours, then within seven days, and then finally within a month to store information in long-term memory. Reintegrate yourself when you forget some things —trace back your path when you read about the now-forgotten topic. Avoid panicking, as it leads to further complications. Study a combo of logical and theoretical subjects in a day to generate interest and enjoy studying. These tips can help you to study and score better. Use them and see the positive changes in yourself.

'*The champions keep playing until they do well.*'

—*Billie Jean King*

Revision is as important as learning new concepts. If revision is not done of the previously learnt things, then the time and efforts spent on learning those things become a waste—as with time, you will forget what you have read. To master anything, you need to revise as much as possible so that the related connections in your brain can become stronger and permanent. The secrets of my performance are continuous practice and revision. Without them, no one can excel.

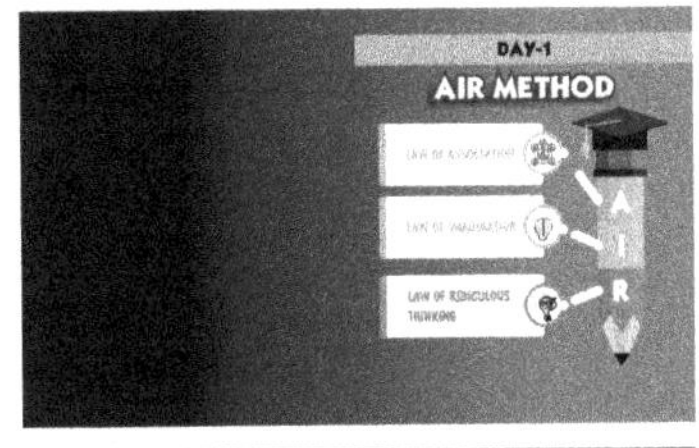

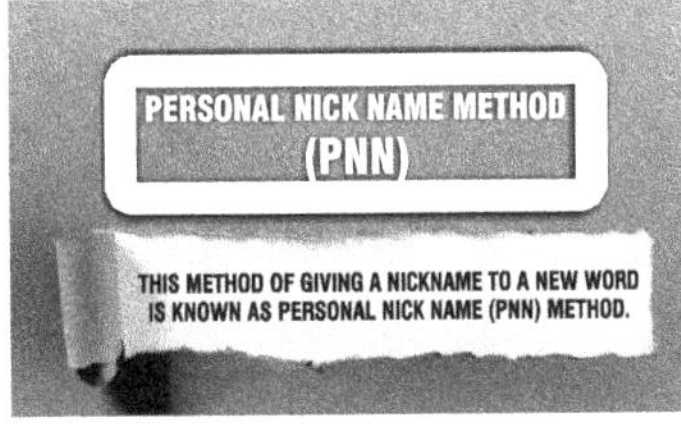

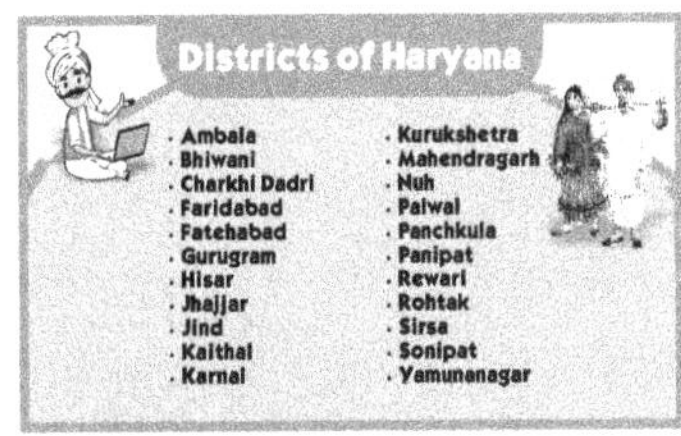

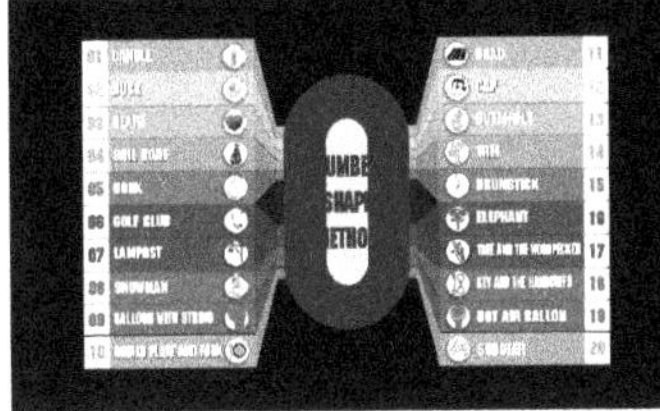

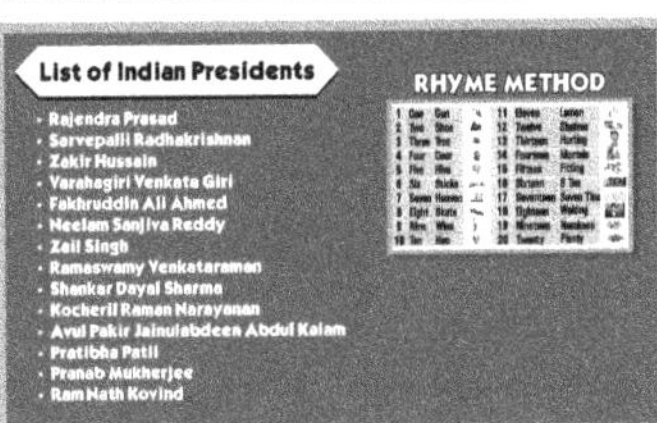

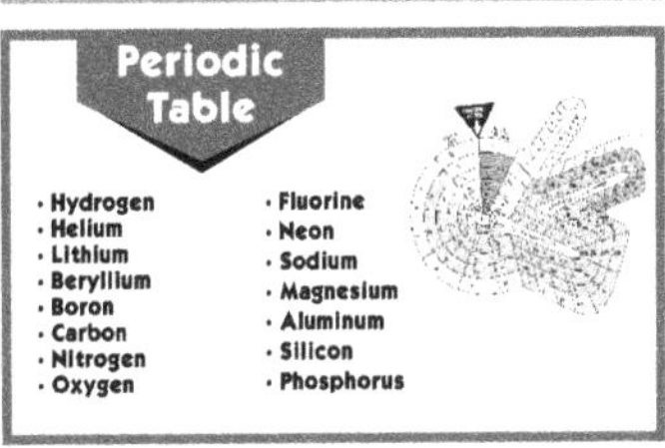

Here is a brief revision of all the previous chapters that you have studied. In the first chapter, you learnt about the association, imagination, and ridiculous thinking (AIR) principles in-depth, with examples like a baby elephant tied with a rope. There, you were told to learn new things like a kid and stay curious and excited throughout this journey. In the second chapter, you got to know about the story or chain method. In that you became aware of the power of stories and memorised random words effortlessly. I am sure you still remember—the chocolate, the person holding it, the vehicle he was sitting on, garden, tiger, MRI machine, etc. In the third chapter, you were introduced to the number shape method, where you associated the shapes of numbers with certain images and used them to memorise shopping lists. In the rhyme method you learnt in chapter four, instead of comparing the shapes of the numbers, you compared the rhythms of the numbers with known words. And with these two methods, you could remember as many as forty items from a list. Then came the PNN method. It acted as a saviour when you encountered pictureless unfamiliar words. It made your learning process interesting and effective.After using those methods, you were able to memorise the lists of Indian presidents and Indian states. Not only this, but you also memorised the districts of Haryana and the periodic table.

With memorisation techniques, you can easily learn various lists and words and make your learning experience highly enjoyable. You have got the keys to success. In case you face difficulties, remember the quote by Maya Angelou, 'You may encounter many defeats, but you must not be defeated. In fact, it may be necessary to encounter the defeats, so you can know who you are, what you can rise from, how you can still come out of it.'

If you want to strengthen your foundation further, you can revisit the previous chapters and spend a few minutes recalling them. It will take less than one-third time to go through them compared to the first time you read them. After this, move forward with more enthusiasm, and josh, memory champ!

'Without a solid foundation, you'll have trouble creating anything of value.'

—*Anonymous*

The major reason for unsatisfactory performance is improper revision. Without efficient revision, the entire effort put into studies can go waste as you won't be able to recollect what you have studied when you need to recall it. Revision boosts confidence and strengthens the neural connection, by which the information gets deeply embedded in your brain. Once you revise what you have learnt in this book, you will be astonished to find out how many new things you have explored and how much you have been benefitted from this book.

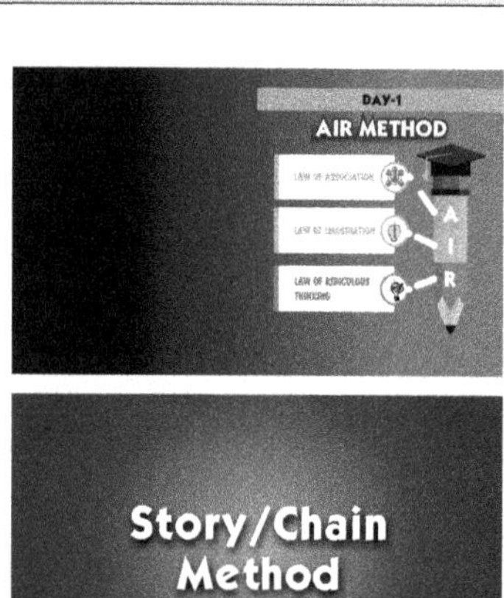

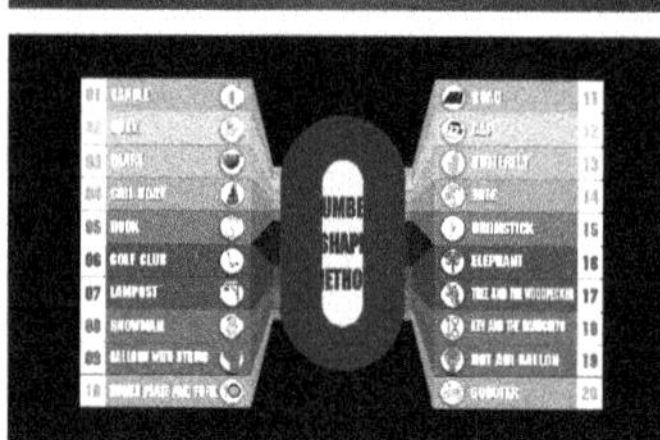

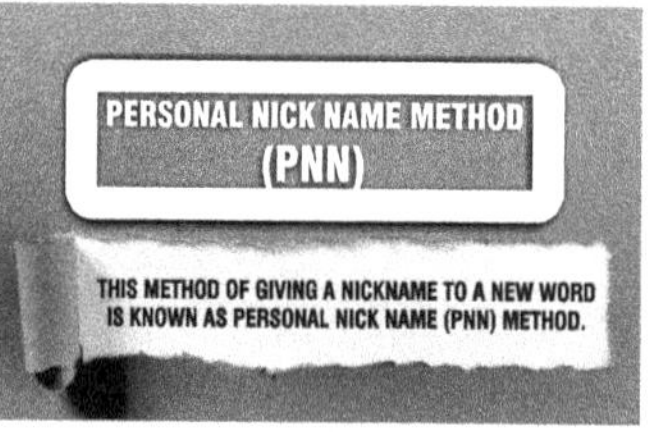

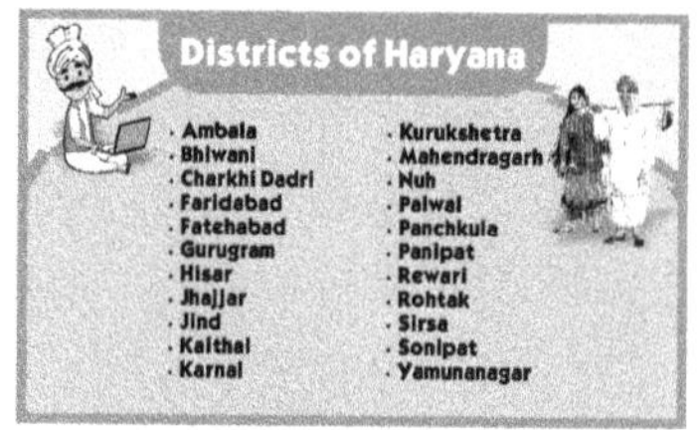

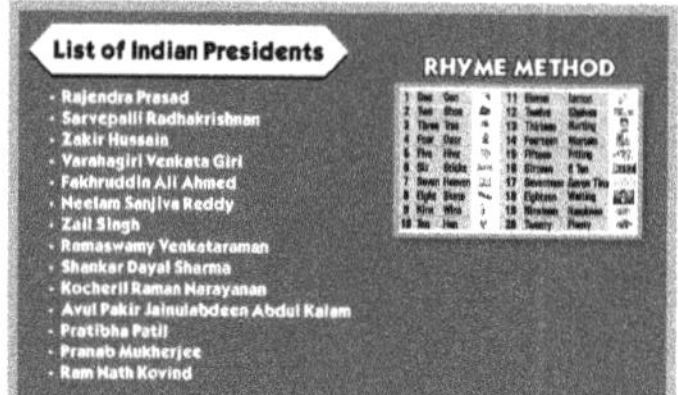

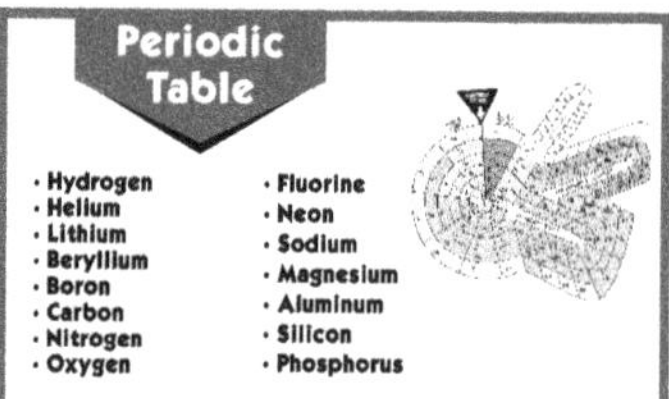

You learnt some very impactful methods that have uncountable applications. First, you got to know about the AIR method in which you associated, imagined, and ridiculously thought about something that you want to memorise. Then came the story method, where you made interesting and entertaining stories. You were able to learn lists of words and recall them in forward, reverse, and random sequences with it. In the number-shape method, you associated the shapes of the numbers with other known shapes. This helped you to remember the exact positions of words in a list. Using the rhyme method, you found out the words that rhymed with different numbers and used them to remember important tasks and appointments. Then came the highly crucial PNN method. It was used to give pictures to pictureless, unknown, or unfamiliar words. This made learning difficult words simpler. Then, you saw the applications of these methods. You learnt the list of Indian presidents, prime ministers, Indian states, districts, the periodic table, etc., in a way you never tried before.

The link method helped you to memorise difficult GK-related information. By using it and other methods, you were able to memorise countries and their currencies; minerals and their places of origin, inventions and their inventors; countries and their capitals, currencies, and continents altogether; books and their authors; states and their capitals; minerals and their places of origin and much more. Then you learnt about the phonetic method. By associating the sounds or codes of numbers, you converted them into meaningful words, which were easy to remember.

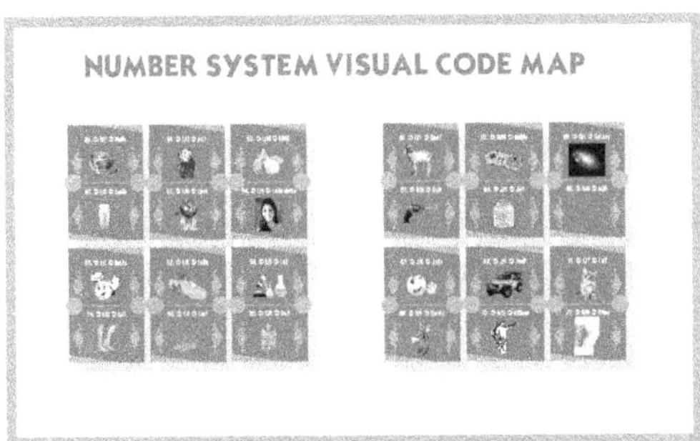

Try To Memorize These Sequence of Complex Number Using Number System Visual Code

51	22	10	54	82
74	88	96	30	52
92	01	37	25	09
61	84	12	04	57
66	52	97	24	56

You got to know the words that can be created for number 01 till number 99 using the phonetic method. Then you saw glimpses of its application by learning a complex sequence of numbers without difficulty.

You must have noticed that you have covered a lot till here. And, if you have studied all this properly, then I can guarantee that along with your memory—your GK, intelligence, IQ, and overall personality must have improved significantly. Now, you can spend one or two days completely revising, reviewing, and recalling what you have studied in this book. Good luck, memory master!